CONTENTS

Level 8

UNIT 1: GOOD THINKING!

UNIT 2: SEE FOR YOURSELF

The Terrible EEK

Two Bad Ants

Opt: An Illusionary Tale

Science Magic

UNIT 3: FAMILY ALBUM

The Patchwork Quilt

How My Parents Learned to Eat

Ramona Forever

On Granddaddy's Farm

CONTENTS
Level 9

UNIT 1: COMMUNITY SPIRIT

UNIT 2: FORCES OF NATURE

UNIT 3: TEAMWORK

Dream Wolf

Operation Rescue: Saving Sea Life From Oil Spills

The Rooster Who Understood Japanese

Turtle Knows Your Name

SENTENCES

Rewrite this colorful paragraph about painting. Make any incomplete sentences complete by adding a subject or a predicate. Also keep an eye out for incorrect punctuation.

Artists bring beauty to our world? Some artists use all the colors of the rainbow. Red, blue, and green. Making circles and squares. Also use many different kinds of paints. Watercolors and oil paints. Many artists draw the world they see around them? Paintings on paper. An artist often begins working at a very young age. There are as many artists as there are people.

_____

_____

_____

_____

_____

_____

_____

_____

_____

_____

_____

_____

_____

Extension: Have students write five sentences that describe things that they would like to draw or paint.

WHAT IS A SENTENCE?

> A **sentence** is a group of words that expresses a complete thought. A **sentence fragment** does not express a complete thought. It is missing either a subject or predicate.
>
> This is a complete sentence: *Many kinds of animals live in Panama.*
>
> This is a sentence fragment: *Many kinds of animals.*

Read the following sentences and sentence fragments. Write *S* next to each complete sentence. Write *F* next to each fragment.

1. _____ Some Panamanian animals are tame, not wild.

2. _____ Dogs, cats, cows, and chickens.

3. _____ The rooster crowed a loud "cock-a-doodle-doo."

4. _____ Many other Panamanian animals.

5. _____ Brightly-colored tree frogs.

6. _____ Sometimes you can see flocks of yellow-and-green parrots in the sky.

7. _____ Lazy brown sloths with three toes.

8. _____ Black toucans with flat, yellow bills.

9. _____ Black, white-faced monkeys make an interesting sight.

10. _____ Jaguars are large, fierce cats that look like leopards.

2

Extension: Have pupils list five of their favorite animals and write a complete sentence telling what is special about each of those animals.

Level 8/Unit 1

10

Macmillan/McGraw-Hill

SUBJECTS IN SENTENCES

> The **complete subject** includes all the words that tell whom or what the sentence is about: *Many wealthy, foreign tourists* visit beautiful Panama each year.
>
> The **simple subject** is the main word or group of words in the complete subject: Many wealthy, foreign *tourists* visit beautiful Panama each year.

Draw a circle around the complete subject. Then write the simple subject of each sentence on the line.

1. Clean, sandy beaches can be found in Panama.

   _____

2. High, rugged mountains can also be found there.

   _____

3. Busy, crowded cities are a part of Panama, too.

   _____

4. The rain forest is a very interesting place. _____

5. Jaguars slink through the rain forest. _____

6. Colorful flowers attract birds and insects. _____

7. Many insects can be found there. _____

8. One danger is that rain forests may be cut down.

   _____

9. Many people are working to protect rain forests.

   _____

10. Everyone must work together to save the forests.

    _____

Extension: Have students work in pairs. Ask one student to write five sentences about rain forests or about Panama. Then ask the other student to underline the simple subject in each sentence. Have students switch roles and repeat the activity.

PREDICATES IN SENTENCES

> The **complete predicate** includes all the words that tell what the subject does or is:
> Sloths *move very slowly.*
>
> The **simple predicate** is the main word or group of words in the complete predicate:
> Sloths *move* very slowly.

Draw a line under the complete predicate. Then write the simple predicate of each sentence on the line.

1. Sloths live in Central and South America. _____

2. They spend most of their time high in the trees.

   _____

3. They hang upside down from tree branches.

   _____

4. Sloths eat the tender leaves of Cecropia trees.

   _____

5. A Cecropia tree has shiny gray bark on its trunk.

   _____

6. Its leaves grow as big as the page of a newspaper.

   _____

7. Sloths come to the ground to get to another tree.

   _____

8. They swim quite well if they need to. _____

9. The word *sloth* means "unwillingness to work."

   _____

Extension: Ask students to write the subject part of a sentence on a sheet of paper. Have students exchange papers and write a predicate to make a complete sentence. Then have them underline the simple predicate.

Macmillan/McGraw-Hill

PUNCTUATING SENTENCES

> A **complete sentence** ends with some kind of punctuation. The punctuation can be a period, a question mark, or an exclamation mark.
>
> A **period** comes at the end of a statement: I like to draw and paint.
>
> A **question mark** is found after a question: Do you like drawing?
>
> An **exclamation mark** follows an expression of strong feelings:
>
> That's a terrific picture!

Edit the following sentences correctly. Use the correct capitalization and end punctuation.

1. i think animals are hard to draw

2. do you think this really looks like a bird

3. i've never seen an eagle

4. have you ever seen one

5. sometimes it's easier to draw something you're looking at

6. why don't you draw a picture of me

7. then I'll draw a picture of you

8. do I really look like that

9. that's a great picture

10. is that an eagle sitting on my shoulder

Extension: Have students work in pairs to look through magazines to find examples of the different kinds of end punctuation. Have them copy an example of each.

TYPES OF SENTENCES

Add a capital letter and the correct end punctuation for each sentence in the following paragraph.

did you know Jane's birthday is on July 4th _____ july

4th is not just Jane's birthday _____ it's also the birthday of

the United States _____ the United States of America

began on July 4, 1776 _____ don't you think that Jane's

birthday is special _____ birthdays are really wonderful

_____ our family celebrates birthdays with cake _____

let's celebrate now _____ we can celebrate our un-

birthdays _____ is this a happy un-birthday to us _____

Extension: Have pupils write four things that they usually do to celebrate their own birthdays. Then have them write a statement, a question, a command, and an exclamation about birthdays.

Level 8/Unit 1

20

WHAT ARE THE FOUR TYPES OF SENTENCES?

There are four basic types of sentences.
  A **statement** is a sentence that tells something.
  A **question** is a sentence that asks something.
  A **command** is a sentence that tells or asks someone to do something.
  An **exclamation** is a sentence that shows strong feeling.

Read each sentence below. On the line after each sentence, write the type of sentence it is: *statement, question, command,* or *exclamation.*

1. Ginkgo trees first came from China. _____

2. They are now also grown in the United States.

  _____

3. Many cities have planted ginkgo trees. _____

4. They can grow in city smog where many trees can't.

  _____

5. Can you recognize a ginkgo tree? _____

6. Look at these leaves. _____

7. They're leaves from a ginkgo tree. _____

8. Aren't the leaves pretty? _____

9. Fossil prints of ginkgo leaves have been found.

  _____

10. Do you know that they lived millions of years ago?

  _____

10   Level 8/Unit 1

Extension: Have students choose a tree or flower and write at least eight sentences about it, including two examples of each of the four kinds of sentences.

7

STATEMENTS AND QUESTIONS

> A **statement** is a sentence that tells something. It ends with a period.
>
> A **question** is a sentence that asks something. It ends with a question mark.

On the line after each sentence, write *statement* or *question* for the kind of sentence it is. On the line below, write the sentence correctly. Add the correct capitalization and end punctuation.

1. many people live in cities _____

   _____

2. the cities are run by electricity _____

   _____

3. electricity lights the houses and streets _____

   _____

4. what is it like when the electricity goes out _____

   _____

5. if it's at night, the whole city is dark _____

   _____

6. if you're at home, it seems like a different place _____

   _____

7. has that ever happened to you _____

   _____

8. were you in a city at night when the lights went out _____

   _____

Extension: Have students pair up, choose a subject, and then take turns making up statements and questions about that subject. The student who is not making the sentence tells what kind of sentence was given.

COMMANDS AND EXCLAMATIONS

A **command** is a sentence that tells someone to do something. The subject of the sentence is understood. The end punctuation can be a period or an exclamation mark.

An **exclamation** is a sentence that shows strong feeling. It ends with an exclamation mark.

On the line after each sentence, write *command* or *exclamation* for the kind of sentence it is. On the line below, write the sentence correctly. Add the correct capitalization and end punctuation.

1. the electricity has gone out _____

_____

2. watch out _____

_____

3. be careful not to trip over anything _____

_____

4. i can't see my hand in front of my face _____

_____

5. try to find the candles _____

_____

6. find a flashlight _____

_____

7. the batteries don't work _____

_____

8. let's keep calm _____

_____

Macmillan/McGraw-Hill

Extension: Have students write two commands and two exclamations to tell about some kind of emergency situation.

FOUR TYPES OF SENTENCES

On the line after each sentence, write *statement, question, command,* or *exclamation* to tell the kind of sentence it is. On the line below, write the sentence correctly. Remember to add a capital letter and end punctuation.

1. do you have a favorite story _____

_____

2. tell it to me _____

_____

3. would you like to hear what my favorite is _____

_____

4. i like to read stories about real people _____

_____

5. listen to this _____

_____

6. this is a terrific story _____

_____

7. i just finished reading the whole book _____

_____

8. would you like to read it too _____

_____

9. you won't believe the ending _____

_____

Extension: Write the names of each of the four types of sentences on separate slips of paper. Have students take turns drawing a slip and then writing a sentence of that type.

SUBJECTS AND PREDICATES

Read the following paragraphs about animals. Rewrite the paragraphs and add words to each sentence to make it more descriptive and vivid. Make the sentences roar to life!

Giraffes have necks. Their eyes are rimmed with eyelashes. Giraffes can see better. A giraffe's lips grasp and hold to help them eat leaves. Every giraffe has horns.

Our family likes the zoo. The snakes are in the reptile house. Snakes slither. The lions were roaring. Three wolves howled. The camel and its baby played. The peacocks strutted.

_____

_____

_____

_____

_____

_____

_____

_____

_____

_____

_____

_____

_____

Macmillan/McGraw-Hill

WHAT ARE SUBJECTS AND PREDICATES? FRAGMENTS?

A **complete sentence** has both a subject and a predicate. If it has only one and not the other, it is a fragment. It is not a complete sentence.

The **complete subject** of a sentence includes all the words that tell whom or what the sentence is about.
> *That long, needle-thin body* belongs to a dragonfly.

The **complete predicate** of a sentence includes all the words that tell what the subject does or is.
> Many people *call dragonflies "darning needles."*

Draw one line under each complete subject. Draw two lines under each complete predicate.

1. The four silver-colored wings of a dragonfly are never folded.

2. A dragonfly's wings help it zoom through the air.

3. A dragonfly keeps looking for food.

4. It is known as the hawk of the insect world.

5. Other insects are caught and eaten by the dragonfly in flight.

Complete each of the following sentence fragments about insects. Write either a complete subject or a complete predicate.

6. Mosquitoes _____

7. _____ tried to sting me.

8. The beautiful butterfly _____

9. All the ants in the anthill _____

10. _____ was hidden under the leaf.

Extension: Have students list as many insects as possible. Then have them pair off. Have students, using their lists, take turns making a complete sentence about each insect: one student giving a complete subject and the other finishing with the predicate.

12

Level 8/Unit 1

10

Macmillan/McGraw-Hill

SUBJECTS IN SENTENCES

> The **complete subject** includes all the words that tell whom or what the sentence is about.
>
> > *Many people* enjoy bird watching.
>
> The **simple subject** is the main word or group of words in the complete subject.
>
> > Many *people* enjoy bird watching.

Draw a circle around the complete subject. Then write the simple subject of each sentence on the line.

1. Serious bird watchers learn a lot by looking at birds.

_____

2. A bird watcher watches birds by being quiet. _____

3. Fancy equipment is not needed for bird watching.

_____

4. A pair of binoculars sometimes helps. _____

5. Many birds can be seen, even in a large city.

_____

6. Two friends walked quietly through a park. _____

7. Seven Canada geese flew overhead. _____

8. The fast-flying birds disappeared quickly. _____

9. A large woodpecker peeked its head out of a hole.

_____

10. It continued to tap, tap, tap a hole in the old tree.

_____

Macmillan/McGraw-Hill

PREDICATES IN SENTENCES

> The **complete predicate** includes all the words that tell what the subject of a sentence does or is.
>
> The animals in the cat family *fascinate people.*
>
> The **simple predicate** is the main word or group of words in the complete predicate.
>
> The animals in the cat family *fascinate* people.

Draw a circle around the complete predicate. Then write on the line the simple predicate of each sentence.

1. House cats lived with people in ancient times.

   _____

2. All cats have a reputation for being free and independent.

   _____

3. Some cats are known for being fierce, too. _____

4. Small house cats look like tigers. _____

5. Huge tigers pounce on their prey. _____

6. House cats jump suddenly on their prey, too. _____

7. Outdoor cats kill mice and birds. _____

8. Playful cats play serious games with a piece of string.

   _____

9. Cats and kittens walk quietly on padded feet.

   _____

10. They surprise the people that they live with. _____

Extension: Ask students to write the subject part of a sentence on a sheet of paper. Have students exchange their papers and write a predicate to make a complete sentence. Have them underline the simple predicate.

Macmillan/McGraw-Hill

COMPOUND SUBJECTS AND PREDICATES IN SENTENCES

A **compound subject** is two or more simple subjects that have the same predicate. The simple subjects are joined by the word *and*.

> Our *dog and cat* do not fight with each other.

A **compound predicate** is two or more simple predicates that have the same subject. The simple predicates are joined by *and*.

> The two animals *sleep and eat* very nicely together.

Draw a line under each compound subject. Circle each compound predicate.

1. Mary and Dan visited a farm over the summer.
2. The people laughed and cried during the play.
3. The bug hopped and flew out of the room.
4. Lions and tigers both eat meat.
5. The nest and eggs fell out of the tree.
6. We ate and played games at the picnic.
7. The ducks and geese flew away from the pond.
8. The class read and reread the story.
9. Both newspapers and television report the news.
10. The pots and pans are dirty.

Part of a compound subject or predicate is missing from each sentence. Complete each subject or predicate with something that makes sense.

11. I washed and _____ my hands after playing.

12. Cake and _____ are nice for a birthday party.

13. April and _____ are good months for planting.

14. The children jumped and _____ with happiness.

Extension: Have students write *CS* for compound subject or *CP* for compound predicate beside sentences 11–14 above.

SENTENCE COMBINING

Read the paragraph. Rewrite it and combine each pair of short sentences into one longer sentence.

> Nancy walked on the beach. Tom walked on the beach. They found some seashells. They picked up some seashells. Some of the shells were pink. Others were yellow and white. The children walked. The children swam. The sunshine felt wonderful. The water was cold. Nancy and Tom loved being at the beach. They enjoyed finding the shells.

_____

_____

_____

_____

_____

_____

Wish You Were Here!

Imagine you are on vacation at the seashore of your dreams. First, decide where you are. Then write a postcard to the folks back home. Write about all the things you want to see and do. When you reread your postcard, combine sentences if you can.

_____

_____

_____

_____

_____

Extension: Have students pair off and choose a favorite seashore to write about. Have them write two related sentences and then use *and* or *but* to join the sentences.

16

Level 8/Unit 1

Macmillan/McGraw-Hill

SENTENCE COMBINING: *AND*

> You can show that ideas are linked by using a conjunction. A **conjunction** is a word such as *and.* Two related sentences can be joined with a comma and *and.*
>
> SEPARATE: We don't live near the sea. I've never even been to the seashore.
>
> COMBINED: We don't live near the sea, *and* I've never even been to the seashore.

Combine each of the following pairs of sentences. Use a comma and the conjunction *and.*

1. I've dreamed of going to the seashore. Someday I'll go there.

_____

2. "Sea Fever" is a poem by John Masefield. It begins, "I must go down to the sea again, to the lonely sea and the sky."

_____

_____

3. I would like to go to the sea. The poem says something about how I feel.

_____

4. Masefield used *lonely* to describe the sea. That's how I would describe it.

_____

5. Most of our world is covered by water. The seas are filled with living things.

_____

6. My friend went to the beach. She brought back seashells.

_____

Macmillan/McGraw-Hill

Extension: Have students write two related sentences about the sea and then use the word *and* to join them.

SENTENCE COMBINING: BUT

> When ideas in separate sentences are linked, you can connect them to make one sentence. You can use the conjunction *and* to show two related ideas. You can use the conjunction *but* to show two *contrasting* ideas.
>
> Use the conjunction *and* or *but* to connect two sentences. Remember to use a comma before *and* or *but*.
>
> Use *and* to combine two similar ideas.
>
> SEPARATE: New ways for exploring underwater are being found. New equipment for underwater exploration is being made.
>
> COMBINED: New ways for exploring underwater are being found, *and* new equipment for underwater exploration is being made.
>
> Use *but* to link two contrasting ideas.
>
> SEPARATE: Water covers almost 70 percent of our planet. Less than 10 percent of the oceans have been explored.
>
> COMBINED: Water covers almost 70 percent of our planet, *but* less than 10 percent of the oceans have been explored.

Combine each pair of sentences below. Use the word *and* or *but* and write the new sentence on the line.

1. Scuba gear is one way to explore underwater. Jim Suits are another.

   _____

2. Jim Suits allow a person to dive deeper than scuba gear. They are slow and awkward.

   _____

   _____

3. Tiny submarines could dive deep. They could also travel fast.

   _____

   _____

4. Deep in the ocean it is very dark. Submarines need lights to explore.

   _____

Extension: Have students write two pairs of related sentences about ocean exploration and then use *and* or *but* to join each pair.

4

COMBINING SENTENCES WITH TWO SUBJECTS

> If two sentences have the same **predicate,** they can be combined by joining the **subjects:**
>
> SEPARATE: *Sharks* are dangerous sea animals. *Moray eels* are dangerous sea animals.
>
> COMBINED: *Sharks and moray eels* are dangerous sea animals.

Combine the subjects of the sentences. Write the complete new sentence.

1. White sharks have attacked people. Sand tiger sharks have attacked people. _____

2. Hammerhead sharks have unusual heads. Swordfish have unusual heads. _____

3. Dolphins are not fish. Whales are not fish.

   _____

4. Puffers increase their size by inflating their bodies. Balloonfish increase their size by inflating their bodies.

   _____

5. Seahorses have unusual shapes. Pipefish have unusual shapes.

   _____

6. Red snappers taste great. Yellowtail snappers taste great.

   _____

7. Butterfly fish are brightly colored. Angelfish are brightly colored.

   _____

8. Tuna swim in large schools. Herring swim in large schools.

   _____

Extension: Have students pair off. One student thinks of a sentence with a simple subject. The other student then tries to extend the sentence by making a compound subject with *and* and an appropriate noun.

COMBINING SENTENCES WITH TWO PREDICATES

If two sentences have the same **subject,** they can be combined by joining the **predicates:**

> SEPARATE: Whale sharks *live in the open sea.* Whale sharks *are the largest fish in the world.*

> COMBINED: Whale sharks *live in the open sea and are the largest fish in the world.*

Combine the predicates of each of these sentences. Write the new sentence.

1. Lionfish are brightly striped. Lionfish have poisonous spines. _____

_____

2. Moray eels have thick, leathery skin. Moray eels are armed with knifelike

teeth. _____

_____

3. Parrotfish have unusual teeth. Parrotfish got their name because they

have beaklike jaws. _____

_____

4. Balloonfish can inflate themselves with water or air. Balloonfish swell up

to scare away anything dangerous. _____

_____

5. Sea horses are poor swimmers. Sea horses blend in with underwater

plants to hide from their enemies. _____

_____

20

Extension: Have students pair off. One student thinks of a sentence with a simple predicate. The other student then tries to extend the sentence by making a compound predicate with *and* and an appropriate verb.

Level 8/Unit 1   5

Macmillan/McGraw-Hill

NOUNS

The writer of this letter didn't check it over for mistakes. As you read the letter, correct any errors you find. Look for mistakes made with common nouns, proper nouns, titles, and abbreviations.

Dear Mom,

These last two weeks have gone really fast. I don't believe Summer is almost over, and I'll be home in just a few Days. I can't imagine life without camp, the friends I've made, and the things I've learned.

When I get home, I'm going to visit doctor bennett. She'll know what I have to do to become a Veterinarian. That's what I want to be. I found out when we took care of the horses on Lookout mountain.

Does School start before or after labor day? If it's after, maybe we can visit my friend Mrs campbell. She lives just a short way from us on peach street.

Take care. I'll see you on monday in michigan city.

Extension: Have students take turns composing sentences that include things they would write home about. Ask them to use common nouns, proper nouns, titles, and abbreviations.

WHAT IS A NOUN?

> A **noun** is a word that names a person, place, or thing.

person: brother   **place:** home   **thing:** book

Write all the nouns in each sentence on the line next to that sentence.

1. My favorite meal is breakfast. _____

2. My dad makes great pancakes. _____

3. Pancakes are also called "hotcakes." _____

4. My sister eats lunch at school. _____

5. Lunch might be a sandwich and an apple. _____

6. Our other meals are made at home. _____

7. Our family eats dinner together. _____

8. My grandmother cooks on the stove. _____

9. The children usually drink milk. _____

10. Cookies taste good for dessert. _____

On the lines below, write nouns that fit into each group.

kinds of furniture   **people in families**

11. _____   16. _____

12. _____   17. _____

13. _____   18. _____

14. _____   19. _____

15. _____   20. _____

Extension: Have students list nouns that belong in the following categories: animals, sports, occupations.

Macmillan/McGraw-Hill

COMMON NOUNS

A **common noun** names any person, place, or thing. A common noun is usually not capitalized unless it is the first word of a sentence.

person: gardener   **place:** zoo   **thing:** flower

Complete each sentence with a common noun that makes sense.

1. Everyone likes to eat _____ .

2. Would you like a red or a blue _____ ?

3. We went to the _____ today.

4. Do you have a _____ that I can use?

5. We bought a _____ at the store.

6. I've never seen a purple _____ before.

7. Which _____ do you like best?

8. We ate in the _____ yesterday.

9. I broke my _____ at school.

10. I don't have enough _____ to finish.

On the lines below, write nouns that fit into each group.

types of clothing	**rooms of a house**
11. _____	**16.** _____
12. _____	**17.** _____
13. _____	**18.** _____
14. _____	**19.** _____
15. _____	**20.** _____

20 Level 8/Unit 2

Extension: Have students work with a partner to list five common nouns in each of the categories of person, place, or thing.

PROPER NOUNS

A **common noun** names any person, place, or thing. A **proper noun** names a particular person, place, or thing. A proper noun is always capitalized: Ms. Carter, Dallas, Monday.

Find each proper noun. Write the correct capital letter above it.

1. state
2. pacific ocean
3. month
4. day
5. japan

6. snake river
7. holiday
8. april
9. flag day
10. country

11. ocean
12. california
13. river
14. july
15. wednesday

Next to each common noun, write a proper noun that could replace it.

16. woman _____

17. city _____

18. book _____

19. song _____

20. ocean _____

21. team _____

22. road _____

23. lake _____

24. holiday _____

25. school _____

Extension: Have students work with a partner to list five common nouns and then five proper nouns in each of the categories of person, place, or thing.

Macmillan/McGraw-Hill

TITLES AND ABBREVIATIONS

A **title** is attached to a person's name. It shows an honor, rank, or office. A title always begins with a capital letter. An **abbreviation** is a shortened form of a word. Some abbreviations begin with a capital letter, but they almost always end with a period.

Titles	Measurements	Time	Addresses
Reverend/Rev.	pint/pt.	minute/min.	Street/St.
Doctor/Dr.	pound/lb.	Sunday/Sun.	Road/Rd.
Senator/Sen.	gallon/gal.	January/Jan.	Avenue/Ave.
Mister/Mr.	inch/in.	before noon/A.M.	Court/Ct.
Governor/Gov.	feet/ft.	after noon/P.M.	Place/Pl.

Rewrite each of the following items. Use the abbreviation of the word or words in parentheses.

1. (doctor) Jane Proudfoot _____

2. (Monday), (March) 17 _____

3. 931 Pine (road) _____

4. (senator) Lynn Potter _____

5. (Mister) Joseph Green _____

6. (Governor) Washington _____

7. 4 (feet), 6 (inches) _____

8. 3:00 (in the afternoon) _____

9. (January) 1999 _____

10. (Saturday), (August) 8 _____

10   Level 8/Unit 2

Extension: Have students work in pairs. One student writes ten words that can be abbreviated. The other student writes their abbreviations. Then they reverse roles.

25

Macmillan/McGraw-Hill

PLURAL NOUNS

The writer of this story was in a hurry yesterday, and he or she didn't finish checking the story. As you read, correct any errors you find. Pay attention to singular and plural nouns.

We went on a picnics yesterday. There were four peoples and a zillion ant. An ant may be little, but there are a lot of them.

Our family went to the parks, and we took our lunch. It was delicious! We had apples, sandwich, peachs, and carrot. The best part of the picnic was the cupcake. We left them in a boxes. We shouldn't have done that.

I never had the chance to sink my teeths into even one cupcake. The ants found the cupcakes before we did. Dad was startled by the ants. He fell right on the cupcake box. All the cupcake were squashed.

Picnic! Ants! You can have them. All I'd like is a cupcake.

Extension: Have students work in pairs. One student lists the things they would take on a picnic. The partner converts each singular to a plural noun.

Level 8/Unit 2

12

WHAT IS A PLURAL NOUN?

A **singular noun** names only one person, place, or thing.

A **plural noun** names more than one person, place, or thing.

Add **s** to form the plural of most nouns.

hat   *hats*   plate   *plates*

Write the plural form of each noun.

1. shadow _____

2. leg _____

3. house _____

4. lake _____

5. peak _____

6. desk _____

7. ledge _____

8. movie _____

9. wall _____

10. pool _____

Write the plural form of each noun in parentheses.

11. I'm going to plant (flower) _____ in the garden.

12. There have been lots of (storm) _____ lately.

13. I hope the (rain) _____ don't come today.

14. I like walking in the (wood) _____.

15. Hiking through the (mountain) _____ is great.

16. Swimming across rivers and (lake) _____ is fun, too.

Extension: Have students write five sentences using each of the following words in plural form: *Stove, sink, table, chair, floor.*

PLURAL NOUNS WITH *-S* AND *-ES*

Add *-s* to form the plural of most nouns.
Add *-es* to form the plural of nouns that end in *s, sh, ch,* or *x.*
Add *-s* or *-es* to form the plural of each noun.

1. porch _____
2. sled _____
3. fox _____
4. beach _____
5. class _____

6. bunch _____
7. pass _____
8. lamp _____
9. ash _____
10. carrot _____

Write the plural form of each noun in parentheses.

11. My older (brother) _____ moved out of their room.

12. My (parent) _____ said that could be my room.

13. We moved the (bed) _____.

14. Then we cleaned the (desk) _____.

15. We carried out (box) _____ of stuff.

16. We painted the walls the color of (peach) _____ and cream.

17. We moved in my (book) _____.

18. I found (place) _____ for all my things.

19. My shirts and (pant) _____ were in the closet.

20. All my (wish) _____ had come true. I had a room of my own.

Extension: Have students take turns thinking of singular nouns that end in *s, x, ch,* or *sh* and have other students think of the plural of those words.

Macmillan/McGraw-Hill

PLURAL NOUNS WITH *-IES*

A **plural noun** names more than one person, place, or thing. To form the plural of nouns ending with a *vowel* and *y*, add *-s*.

    bay   *bay<u>s</u>*   toy   *toy<u>s</u>*

To form the plural of nouns ending with a *consonant* and *y*, change the *y* to *i* and add *-es*.

    country   *countr<u>ies</u>*   story   *stor<u>ies</u>*

Write the plural form of each noun.

1. cherry _____
2. city _____
3. tray _____
4. party _____
5. holiday _____
6. penny _____
7. puppy _____
8. lady _____
9. key _____
10. worry _____

Write the plural form of each noun in parentheses.

11. I always look forward to (Saturday) _____.

12. They are usually times of wonderful (discovery) _____.

13. Often our family takes (journey) _____ to the country.

14. We walk in the woods, celebrating the (joy) _____ of life.

15. Sometimes the (sky) _____ rain on our happiness.

16. More often, the sun's (ray) _____ warm our hearts.

17. (Berry) _____ taste delicious eaten right from the bush.

18. (Butterfly) _____ outdo the flowers in lovely colors.

Macmillan/McGraw-Hill

Extension: Have students make a chart on their papers with the headings *Singular* and *Plural*. Have them write as many singular nouns as they can that end in a vowel and *y* or a consonant and *y*, and their plurals.

SPECIAL/IRREGULAR PLURAL NOUNS

Some plural nouns do not follow a regular spelling pattern. These nouns form the plural in a different way.

    mouse   mice   tooth   teeth   loaf   loaves

A few nouns have the same singular and plural forms.

    sheep   moose   salmon

Sometimes you need to use a dictionary to find the plural form of a noun.

Write the plural form of each noun.

1. life _____

2. shelf _____

3. woman _____

4. foot _____

5. scissors _____

6. deer _____

7. pants _____

8. wolf _____

9. trout _____

10. man _____

Write the plural form of each word. Then write a sentence that uses each word.

11. goose _____

_____

12. fish _____

_____

13. child _____

_____

14. calf _____

_____

Extension: Have pupils invent a story using all the examples of plural nouns used on this page. Ask a volunteer to give a sentence using the first word—*mice*—and have the next person build the story from that sentence with the next plural.

Macmillan/McGraw-Hill

SINGULAR POSSESSIVE NOUNS

Read these paragraphs about a knight and a castle. As you read, look for ten mistakes in singular possessive nouns. Cross out each error and write the correct spelling above the word. Be careful you don't wind up in the dungeon!

The knight stood at the rivers edge looking at the castle. The knight horse stood quietly at his side. The only sound was the horses munching as it ate some grass. After a while, the knight mounted his horse and rode toward the castle.

The suns brightness made everything sparkle. Colored banners flew from the castles towers. The castle looked welcoming, but its stone walls were still gray and forbidding. The castles gates were open for the day. Townspeople walked in and out, going about their business. A baker bread smelled wonderful. A farmers vegetables looked ripe and ready to eat.

As the knight rode through the gates, he wondered what would happen. Would he find favor with the royal family? Would he be able to talk with the queens soldiers? Or would he be thrown into the dungeon—the dark underground rooms where the king prisoners were kept?

Extension: Have students form singular possessive nouns by thinking of a castle and listing as many singular nouns as they can think of relating to a castle. Then have them turn those words into singular possessive nouns.

WHAT IS A POSSESSIVE NOUN?

A **possessive noun** is a noun that shows who or what owns something. A singular noun that shows ownership is called a **singular possessive noun**.

Add an apostrophe and *s* to a singular noun to make it possessive.

girl   *girl's*   country   *country's*   chair   *chair's*

Write the possessive form of each underlined noun.

1. the pages of my <u>book</u>   my _____ pages

2. the colors of the <u>balloon</u>   the _____ colors

3. the stones of the <u>wall</u>   the _____ stones

4. the face of a <u>tiger</u>   the _____ face

5. the shape of the <u>hat</u>   the _____ shape

6. the windows of the <u>car</u>   the _____ windows

7. the fur of the <u>fox</u>   the _____ fur

8. the steps of the <u>house</u>   the _____ steps

9. the song of the <u>bird</u>   the _____ song

10. the branches of the <u>tree</u>   the _____ branches

Write the correct possessive form of each singular noun in parentheses.

11. Today is my (brother) _____ birthday.

12. He would like the (cake) _____ frosting to be chocolate.

13. He hopes our (family) _____ present will be a jacket.

14. His jacket was stolen from the (school) _____ library.

15. It won't matter to him what the (jacket) _____ colors are.

Macmillan/McGraw-Hill

FORMING SINGULAR POSSESSIVE NOUNS: (' + *s*)

A **possessive noun** shows who or what owns something. A singular noun that shows ownership is called a **singular possessive noun**.

Add an apostrophe and *s* to a singular noun to make it possessive.

Read the lists of things that tell about Serena and her dog Sanchez. Write out each item as a singular possessive noun. Example: *Serena's hat.*

Serena

1. book _____
2. comb _____
3. coat _____
4. room _____

Sanchez

5. food _____
6. dish _____
7. paws _____
8. leash _____

Write out each sentence, adding an apostrophe and *s* to the singular nouns that should show possession.

9. Miguel yard has a fence around it.

_____

10. A neighbor child stood and looked over the fence.

_____

11. The child sister looked over the fence, too.

_____

12. The children were looking at Miguel flowers.

_____

Extension: Have students take turns thinking of a singular noun and then giving the possessive form of that noun.

FORMING SINGULAR POSSESSIVE NOUNS: (' + *s*) TO *s* ENDINGS

A **possessive noun** shows who or what owns something. A singular noun that shows ownership is called a **singular possessive noun**. Add an apostrophe and *s* to a singular noun that ends in *s* to make it possessive.

grass *grass's*

Write a sentence using the possessive form of each underlined noun.

1. the teacher of my <u>class</u>

_____

2. the skirt of the <u>dress</u>

_____

3. the orders of my <u>boss</u>

_____

4. the tires of a <u>bus</u>

_____

5. the color of the <u>moss</u>

_____

6. the hair of <u>Bess</u>

_____

7. the shape of the <u>glass</u>

_____

8. the cities of <u>Texas</u>

_____

Extension: Have students think of an animal and then turn the name of that animal into a singular possessive noun by adding something the animal does. Examples: *a wolf's howl, a bird's song*. Students who think of animals that end in *s* get extra points.

Level 8/Unit 2

8

POSSESSIVE NOUNS

A **possessive noun** shows who or what owns something.

Add an apostrophe and *s* to a singular noun to make it possessive.

Write a story about a surprise party that a third-grade class gave for one of its members. Use the singular possessive form of at least five of the nouns below.

1. party   **3.** candle   **5.** teacher   **7.** present

2. class   **4.** card   **6.** principal   **8.** cake

_____

_____

_____

_____

_____

_____

_____

_____

_____

_____

_____

_____

_____

Extension: Have students write their names on pieces of paper and then turn them into possessive nouns by adding *'s* and something they have or would like to own. Example: *Pat's horse.* The possessives could then be illustrated.

PLURAL POSSESSIVE NOUNS

Read the following paragraphs about mirrors. As you read, look for ten mistakes in plural possessive nouns. Find each mistake and write the correct spelling above it.

For thousands of years, people mirrors were quiet pools of

water. Then, people began to polish metal. Mirrors were made of

brass, silver, bronze, and gold. Finally, thin coatings of silver were

put on mirrors backs. This made mirrors easier to make and less

costly to buy.

Today, people still look at themselves in mirrors, of course.

Mirrors are also used in many other ways. Rearview mirrors in cars

make driving safer. Dentists mirrors let them look into hard-to-see

places in people mouths. Submarines periscopes let subs stay

underwater while letting them see above water.

Highly polished metal mirrors are still in use. Scientists ideas put

telescopes mirrors to work. Mirrors help us to see and photograph

faraway stars light. Flashlights and headlights have built-in mirrors.

So do lamps in lighthouses. Do mirrors images change people lives?

They certainly make our lives easier and safer.

36

Extension: Have pupils think of things that can be seen in a mirror and list those things in the form of plural nouns. Then ask them to turn those words into plural possessive nouns.

Level 8/Unit 2

10

WHAT IS A PLURAL POSSESSIVE NOUN?

A **possessive noun** shows who or what owns something. A plural noun that shows ownership is a **plural possessive noun.**

Add an apostrophe to make most plural nouns possessive: the *books'* pages

Add an apostrophe and *s* to form the possessive of plural nouns that do not end in *s*:

the *children's* toys

Write the possessive form of each underlined noun.

1. the buttons of the <u>shirts</u>   the _____ buttons

2. the peaks of the <u>mountains</u>   the _____ peaks

3. the colors of the <u>stones</u>   the _____ colors

4. the sizes of the <u>shells</u>   the _____ sizes

5. the footprints of the <u>foxes</u>   the _____ footprints

6. the wings of the <u>planes</u>   the _____ wings

7. the laughter of the <u>women</u>   the _____ laughter

8. the books of the <u>brothers</u>   the _____ books

9. the roofs of the <u>houses</u>   the _____ roofs

10. the eyes of the <u>deer</u>   the _____ eyes

Write the correct possessive form of each plural noun in parentheses.

11. It was both (classes) _____ idea to go walking in the woods.

12. On our walk, we found five kinds of (birds) _____ nests.

13. We also saw lots of (deer) _____ hoofprints.

14. The (trees) _____ seeds were scattered over the ground.

14

Level 8/Unit 2

Extension: Have students write the plural possessive form of each of the following nouns: *sheep, horses, men, fish, insects,* and *mice.* Then have students use three of those plural possessive nouns in sentences.

FORMING PLURAL POSSESSIVE NOUNS (ADDING ' TO S ENDINGS)

A **possessive noun** is a noun that shows who or what owns something. A plural noun that shows ownership is a **plural possessive noun.**

Add an apostrophe to form the possessive of plural nouns that end in *s*:

the *dogs'* barks   the *tables'* legs

Write the possessive form of each underlined noun.

1. the leaves of the <u>tree</u>   the _____ leaves

2. the lives of the <u>animals</u>   the _____ lives

3. the cries of the <u>kittens</u>   the _____ cries

4. the skins of the <u>potatoes</u>   the _____ skins

5. the drawers of the <u>desk</u>   the _____ drawers

6. the heads of the <u>wolves</u>   the _____ heads

7. the riders of the <u>bus</u>   the _____ riders

8. the paws of the <u>puppies</u>   the _____ paws

9. the wishes of the <u>girls</u>   the _____ wishes

10. the roofs of the <u>houses</u>   the _____ roofs

Write the possessive form of each noun in parentheses.

11. The (girls) rooms are going to be cleaned today. _____

12. The (desks) drawers will be emptied and sorted. _____

13. The (bookcases) shelves will be dusted. _____

14. The (pictures) frames will be dusted, too. _____

Extension: Have children write on slips of paper plural nouns that end in *s*. Invite each pupil to draw a slip from a container and then compose a sentence changing the plural noun to a possessive plural.

FORMING PLURAL POSSESSIVE NOUNS (ADDING ' + *s* TO NON-*S* ENDINGS)

> A **possessive noun** shows who or what owns something. A plural noun that shows ownership is a **plural possessive noun**.
>
> Add an apostrophe and *s* to form the possessive of plural nouns that do not end in *s*:
>
> the *men's* thoughts the *women's* ideas

Write the possessive form of each underlined noun.

1. the tails of the <u>mice</u> the _____ tails

2. the horns of the <u>cattle</u> the _____ horns

3. the yells of the <u>children</u> the _____ yells

4. the fillings of the <u>teeth</u> the _____ fillings

5. the toes of the <u>feet</u> the _____ toes

6. the honks of the <u>geese</u> the _____ honks

7. the calves of the <u>moose</u> the _____ calves

8. the eyes of the <u>sheep</u> the _____ eyes

9. the hides of the <u>oxen</u> the _____ hides

10. the trails of the <u>deer</u> the _____ trails

Choose four of the plural nouns used in the above exercise. Then write a sentence that uses each word as a possessive plural noun.

11. _____

12. _____

13. _____

14. _____

Extension: Have students think of as many plural nouns as possible that do not end in *s* and write each on a separate slip of paper. Have pupils compose sentences by drawing a noun from a container and changing the plural noun to a possessive plural.

PLURAL POSSESSIVE NOUNS

A **plural possessive noun** shows that two or more people or things own or have something.

Add an apostrophe to make most plural nouns possessive.

Add an apostrophe and an *s* to make the possessive form of plural nouns that don't end in *s*.

Change each of the following nouns to the plural possessive form. Write the plural possessive form in the blank.

1. child _____
2. rainbow _____
3. mouse _____
4. wolf _____
5. cat _____

6. moose _____
7. city _____
8. day _____
9. box _____
10. hike _____

Write an advertisement for a summer vacation spot. Use at least five plural nouns to show possession.

_____
_____
_____
_____
_____
_____
_____
_____

Extension: Have students find examples of ads that incorporate plural possessive nouns.

Macmillan/McGraw-Hill

ACTION VERBS

If you join a baseball team, you'll find that there are many skills to practice. Hitting the ball is just one of them. Read the following story and find the mistakes made with action verbs. Write the correct verb above each mistake. If you can find ten errors, you'll have a home run!

When spring rolls around, there comes a day when it's time to play ball. First, finds your ball, bat, and glove. Then looked for some other people who are ready to play, too.

There are lots of things to practice. You can hits the ball. You can run as if you're running around the bases. You can catched the ball. You can throws the ball to another person. Or you can pitches the ball to someone who will try and hits it.

Because baseball is a team sport, there are many things that you have to practice doing with other people. But there are some things that you can practice alone. You can ran by yourself. You can tossed the ball up in the air and practices batting by yourself. You can never get enough practice, even if you think you're ready for the World Series.

Extension: Have students think about their favorite sports and write five action verbs that relate to that sport. Then have them write five sentences incorporating those verbs.

WHAT IS AN ACTION VERB (1)?

A **verb** tells what happens in a sentence. An **action verb** shows action. It tells what the subject does or did.

Holly *sewed* some clothes with her grandmother.

Read each group of words and underline the action verb in it. On the line below, write a complete sentence using that group of words.

1. plants a vegetable garden

_____

2. flies through the sky

_____

3. ran into the tree

_____

4. started up the hill

_____

5. read our books

_____

6. walk home

_____

7. said to my cousin

_____

8. held the mirror

_____

Macmillan/McGraw-Hill

WHAT IS AN ACTION VERB (2)?

> A **verb** tells what happens in a sentence. An **action verb** shows action. It tells what the subject does or did.
>
> Robert *walked* quietly through the hallway.
> Robert *tiptoed* quietly through the hallway.

Underline the action verb in each group of words. Then replace that action verb with one that is more interesting or colorful. On the line below, write a complete sentence using the new action verb.

1. made a picture

_____

2. climbed a mountain

_____

3. held the paper

_____

4. says hello

_____

5. cleaned the room

_____

6. speaks softly

_____

7. watched the movie

_____

8. rode the horse

_____

Extension: Have students look through books, newspapers, and magazines to find sports articles that describe the actions of players. Have them underline or list the action verbs and share them with the rest of the class.

ACTION VERBS: FILL IN THE BLANKS

Each of the sentences in the paragraph below has a blank in it where a word or words are missing. In parentheses are two choices that could each fit in the sentence. However, only one is a reasonable choice for the situation. Draw a line under each correct choice.

Early this year, my family _____ (planned, finished) a garden. We _____ (hoped, forgot) to plant it last Saturday. But before we _____ (started, weeded), thunder boomed through the air. Lightning _____ (wandered, ripped) through the sky. Rain _____ (pounded, leaked) on the roof. The wind _____ (roared, sighed softly) through the trees. So much rain _____ (fell, was needed) that the garden plot was soon under water. We stayed indoors and _____ (threw out, thought about) what we were going to plant. Dad _____ (helped, decided) to plant roses. The rest of us _____ (wanted, began) to plant vegetables.

Extension: Have students think of a family activity and list five action verbs that tell about that activity. Then have them write sentences about the activity using those action verbs.

44

Level 8/Unit 3

10

Macmillan/McGraw-Hill

ACTION VERBS

Read the paragraphs below. Find five action verbs that should be corrected and write the correction above each error. Then replace five additional verbs with more exact or interesting action verbs.

When we went to the grocery store, we buys several bags of groceries. We puts the bags in a grocery cart and pushed the cart out to our car. Then we lift the bags from the cart to the trunk of the car. When we lifted the last bag, it drop to the ground.

The grocery bag broke and the groceries went all over the place. The peanut butter jar fell on the ground. The bottle of milk bounced. Apples and grapes rolled. Our groceries went in all directions! We moves quickly to pick up things. We were lucky because we saved almost all the food.

Extension: Have students find an interesting action picture in a magazine or newspaper and write at least five sentences about it. Make sure they use action verbs.

PRESENT TENSE

Rice is one of the most important foods in the world. It is especially important in Japan. Read the following paragraphs about the importance of rice in Japanese life. Then proofread the page. Find and mark ten errors made with verbs in the present tense.

Throughout the world, millions of people eats rice as a basic part of their diet. Japan is just one of many countries where rice is important. It is eaten with almost every meal. In fact, the word for *rice* in Japanese is often used to mean *meal*.

For so much rice to be eaten, a lot of rice has to be grown. Growing rice is very hard. It involve everyone on the farm and on all the farms around. In Japan, early summer is the busiest time of year for a rice farmer. Small rice plants are planted in fields that are covered with water. During the summer, the rice plants grows. In the fall, farmers cuts off the water supply to the rice fields. The fields dries out. Then the farmers harvests the rice.

The Japanese people not only eat rice at each meal. They also pounds it to make the rice cakes that are used at parties. They turns rice into a paste and uses it as a glue. The rest of the rice plant is also used. Rice straw provide many things that are used in daily life. Rice straw is made into ropes, sacks, and mats for homes.

Macmillan/McGraw-Hill

Extension: Have students discuss one food they eat more of than any other. Have them write a paragraph about their favorite food. Tell them to write in the present tense—as if the experience is happening now.

SINGULAR SUBJECTS: ADD -S OR -ES

A verb in the **present tense** tells what happens now.

When you use present-tense verbs with a singular subject, add -s to most verbs.

    hop, *hops*   walk, *walks*

Add -es to verbs that end in *s, ch, sh, x,* or *z:*

    mess, *messes*   stitch, *stitches*   fish, *fishes*   mix, *mixes*   buzz, *buzzes*

Change *y* to *i* and add -es to verbs that end in a consonant and *y:*

    fly, *flies*   worry, *worries*

Write the correct present tense of each verb in parentheses.

1. Akiko is a schoolgirl. She (live) in Japan. _____

2. Like most people in Japan, she (own) a bicycle.

    _____

3. Akiko (ride) her bike to school. _____

4. Her father (take) his bike to work. _____

5. Akiko (carry) her books in the bike's basket. _____

6. She (put) her bike in a special parking lot for bikes.

    _____

7. She (hurry) home from school. _____

8. If her bike is broken, Akiko (miss) riding it. _____

9. She (fix) her bike with the help of her parents.

    _____

10. She (like) the color of her bike. _____

Extension: Have students list all the verbs they can think of connected with owning or riding a bike. Then have them use the present tense of those verbs in sentences.

PLURAL SUBJECTS: DO NOT ADD *-s* OR *-es*

A verb in the present tense tells what happens now.

Do not add *-s* or *-es* to a present-tense verb when the subject is plural **or** if the subject is *I* or *you*.

Most people *want* to be polite.

I *like* to be polite, too.

Write the correct present tense of each verb in parentheses.

1. Different countries often (observe, observes) different customs and

   manners. _____

2. Americans usually (shake, shakes) hands when meeting another person.

   _____

3. They (eat, eats) their meals with knives and forks.

   _____

4. They (drink, drinks) soup with a soup spoon.

   _____

5. They (sit, sits) on chairs around a table when eating a meal.

   _____

6. In Japan, people (bow, bows) when they greet each other.

   _____

7. They (use, uses) chopsticks for eating. _____

8. They (swallow, swallows) soup straight from a bowl.

   _____

Extension: Have students discuss table manners. Steer them toward what they should *do* rather than *not do*. List some of the phrases mentioned on the board. Have students choose five verbs and write sentences in the present tense.

Level 8/Unit 3

8

Macmillan/McGraw-Hill

SINGULAR AND PLURAL SUBJECTS

> A verb in the present tense tells what happens now.
>
> When you use present-tense verbs with a singular subject, add *-s* to most verbs.
>
> Add *-es* to verbs that end in *s*, *ch*, *sh*, *x*, or *z*.
>
> Change *y* to *i* and add *-es* to verbs that end in a consonant and *y*.
>
> Do not add *-s* or *-es* to a present-tense verb when the subject is plural or if the subject is *I* or *you*.

Write the correct present tense for each verb in parentheses. Then use the present tense of the verb in a sentence of your own.

1. A bird _____. Birds _____. (fly)

_____

2. A butterfly _____. Butterflies _____. (flutter)

_____

3. A bee _____. Bees _____. (buzz)

_____

4. A snake _____. Snakes _____. (hiss)

_____

5. A bear _____. Bears _____. (growl)

_____

6. A monkey _____. Monkeys _____. (screech)

_____

7. An otter _____. Otters _____. (play)

_____

Macmillan/McGraw-Hill

14 Level 8/Unit 3

Extension: Teach students to play Verbations. Have them make a Verb Box by writing all of the verbs used in this lesson and then putting the cards into a box. Players can reach into the box, take out a card, and use that verb in its present tense in a sentence.

PRESENT TENSE

> A verb in the present tense tells what happens now.
>
> When you use present-tense verbs with a singular subject, add -s to most verbs.
>
> Add -es to verbs that end in s, ch, sh, x, or z.
>
> Change y to i and add -es to verbs that end in a consonant and y.
>
> Do not add -s or -es to a present-tense verb when the subject is plural **or** if the subject is I or you.

Underline the correct verb from the pair in parentheses.

1. Most large cities (plan, plans) parks.

2. A park (help, helps) the people of the city.

3. The green openness (remind, reminds) people of nature.

4. It (give, gives) room to run and play.

5. Parks also (let, lets) people enjoy fresh air.

6. People (enjoy, enjoys) parks for different reasons.

7. A child (play, plays) in the playground.

8. A jogger (run, runs) on the track.

9. Birds and squirrels (find, finds) homes in a park.

10. Flowers (bloom, blooms) for everyone to enjoy.

Write the correct present tense of the verb in parentheses.

1. I _____ to watch the ducks in the park.   (like)

2. They _____ underwater for food.   (dive)

3. Sometimes a duck _____ when it lands in the water. (splash)

4. Usually, it _____ in gracefully.   (glide)

Extension: Have students think about things they enjoy when they go to a park. Have them take turns saying sentences about their favorite activities, using the present tense.

50

Level 8/Unit 3

14

Macmillan/McGraw-Hill

PAST TENSE

What would you like to be when you grow up? Read this story about a zoo veterinarian. Then proofread the page. In each paragraph, find five errors made with verbs in the past tense. Write the correct verb above the error.

Dr. Martin watchhed the tiger closely. The tiger paceed back and forth in its cage, from one corner to another. While it walkked, it roarred one roar right after another. Clearly, the tiger did not want to be in the animal hospital. It wants to be back in its enclosure in the zoo. The enclosure was as much like the tiger's natural home as the zoo could make it.

Dr. Martin likeed the big cats and studyed them closely. She worryed about them as if they were family and loveed working with them. But the thundering sound in the small room hurt Dr. Martin's ears. She knew the tiger was in pain. She had pullled a tiger's tooth before. But when a tiger has a toothache, everyone had better watch out!

Dr. Martin grined suddenly as she rememberred some of the things she had wanted to be when she was growing up. There was a time she longs to be an artist. Then she hopes to be a teacher. And then she couldn't make up her mind whether she wanted to be a pilot or a doctor. As she worked to become a vet, Dr. Martin never lookked back. She knew that was what she wanted to do. Now she just looks forward to taking care of the tiger's toothache.

Macmillan/McGraw-Hill

15

Level 8/Unit 3

Extension: Have students draw up a list of zoo animals and think of action words to describe their voices or actions. Have them use those words in the past tense in sentences: *The tiger roared.*

51

VERBS IN THE PAST: ADD *-ED*

A verb in the **past tense** tells what happened earlier. Add *-ed* to most verbs to show past tense. If a verb ends with an *e*, drop the *e* and add *-ed*.

laugh, *laughed*   smile, *smiled*

In the space, write the past tense for each verb in parentheses. Then write a sentence using the past tense of that verb.

1. Last year, I had to go to the hospital. I _____ all the way there. (yell) _____

2. My brothers and I had been playing. We _____ through the house. (race) _____

3. We _____ out the door and down the stairs. (scramble) _____

4. We _____ to climb a big tree in the backyard. (decide) _____

5. My brothers _____ me to climb the tree first. (dare) _____

6. So I _____ climbing the tree.   (start)

    _____

7. I _____ higher than I ever had before.   (climb)

    _____

8. All of a sudden, I _____ out of the tree. (tumble)

    _____

Extension: Have students list all the verbs on this page under the heading of *Present Tense* or *Past Tense.*

Macmillan/McGraw-Hill

VERBS IN THE PAST: CHANGE Y TO I + -ED

A verb in the past tense tells what happened earlier. Add *-ed* to most verbs to show past tense. If a verb ends with a consonant and *y*, change the *y* to *i* and add *-ed*.

cook, *cooked*   fry, *fried*

In the space, write the past tense for each verb in parentheses. Then write a sentence using the past tense of the verb.

1. If anyone ever asked, Bob _____ that he loved

   dogs. (reply) _____

2. He read and _____ everything he could about

   dogs. (study) _____

3. One day, Bob's mother _____ a puppy home.

   (carry) _____

4. The puppy missed its mother, so it whimpered and _____.

   (cry) _____

5. Bob was overjoyed, but he _____ about the

   puppy. (worry) _____

6. He _____ to find everything the puppy needed.

   (hurry) _____

7. They _____ to feed the puppy. It ate everything.

   (try) _____

8. They took the puppy for a walk in the rain. It _____

   its feet.   (muddy) _____

Extension: Pair off students to make lists of all the verbs they can think of that change the *y* to *i* when adding *-ed*.

Macmillan/McGraw-Hill

VERBS IN THE PAST: DOUBLE THE FINAL CONSONANT + -ED

A verb in the past tense tells what happened earlier. Add -ed to most verbs to show past tense. If a verb ends with one vowel and one consonant, double the consonant and add -ed.

walk, *walked*   trot, *trotted*

In the space provided, write the past tense for each verb in parentheses. Then write a sentence using the past tense of the verb.

1. Sarah wanted to climb a mountain. She and her family _____

   to climb one on their vacation. (plan) _____

2. Before they left, Sarah and her father _____ for

   hiking shoes. (shop) _____

3. At last it was time to leave. Sarah _____ her coat

   and knapsack. (grab) _____

4. She _____ out of the house and into the car.

   (step) _____

5. Sarah's dad asked if she was ready. She _____.

   (grin) _____

6. Then she _____ yes.   (nod) _____

7. Sarah and her family had to drive a long way. At last Sarah's mom

   _____ the car, and they were at their mountain.

   (stop) _____

8. When they started climbing the mountain, Sarah _____

   for a short way.   (skip) _____

Extension: Have students write five sentences about a vacation they liked or a place they can imagine they've been. Remind them to use the past tense as they write.

Level 8/Unit 3

16

Macmillan/McGraw-Hill

PAST TENSE

A verb in the past tense tells what happened earlier.

Add -*ed* to most verbs to show past tense.

If a verb ends with an *e*, drop the *e* and add -*ed*.

If a verb ends with a consonant and *y*, change the *y* to *i* and add -*ed.*

If a verb ends with one vowel and one consonant, double the consonant and add -*ed.*

Write the past tense for each verb in parentheses.

1. Juan and Mary (remember) _____ being little.

2. They (notice) _____ how much they've learned.

3. They (try) _____ to remember the first time they

   did some things, but they couldn't always remember.

4. The first time Mary (whistle), _____ it was very

   special.

5. She (work) _____ hard to learn how to whistle.

6. She even (surprise) _____ herself.

7. Then she (learn) _____ how to play the flute.

8. She (practice) _____ playing every day.

9. Juan (dance) _____ to Mary's music.

10. He (plan) _____ a dance to a certain piece of

    music.

11. Then they (prepare) _____ to show their mother.

12. Juan (worry) _____ that it would look silly.

Extension: Have students think of things they've learned to do. Ask them to list things they've enjoyed learning. Suggest that they use verbs in the past tense.

BE, DO, HAVE

Today, most people live in cities, but many people still live on farms. Even more people think they would like to live on a farm. Read the following story and then proofread it. Find the twelve errors in forms of the verbs *be, do,* and *have.* Write the correct word above the error.

I has always lived in a big city. I are happy living here, but there are times when I start to dream. I dream of being a farmer. What would that be like? My nearest neighbor might be ten or fifteen miles away. I could grow most of my own food. I could see a million stars at night!

Last summer I has the chance to live on a farm. My parents and I was on a farm for two weeks. We do everything a farmer and his family would do. We has to get up early. We fed the chickens and milked the cows. We planted seeds and weeded the garden. We watered the plants. It were amazing the amount of work that had to be done.

We saw a lot of things we had never seen before. We is still thinking about the deer we watched playing in the moonlight. We will always remember how wonderful corn tasted when picked right from the garden. And we never will forget how bright the stars looked at night.

It were a lot of hard work. There was never a time when all the work was finished. There was always more work that had to be done. I be very happy we stayed at the farm. So is my parents. But we was also very happy to come back to our home in the city.

56

Extension: Have students discuss what they imagine life is like on a farm or what they know life to be like there. Then have them write two sentences using a form of *be, do,* or *have.*

Level 8/Unit 3

12

Macmillan/McGraw-Hill

USING *BE*

Subjects and verbs in sentences must agree in number. If the subject is singular, the verb must be singular. If the subject is plural, the verb must be plural.

Am, is, are, was, and *were* are all forms of the word *be.*
Use *am* and *was* with the subject *I.*
   I am hardly ever late for breakfast. *I was* late yesterday.
Use *is* and *was* with *he, she,* or *it.*
   Today *she is* late. *It was* not her fault.
Use *are* and *were* with plural subjects and *you.*
   You are eating breakfast now. *Coretta and Bill are* coming soon.

Read each incomplete sentence and the verbs in parentheses. Then write the verb that correctly completes each sentence.

1. Breakfast _____ an important meal. (is, are)

2. I _____ always ready for breakfast. (am, is)

3. My sister and I _____ waiting for you. (was, were)

4. I _____ going to eat milk, cereal, and fruit. (am, are)

5. We _____ hoping to have pancakes. (was, were)

6. The stove _____ not working right. (was, were)

7. So we _____ not going to have pancakes today. (is, are)

8. The fruit _____ not ripe enough to eat. (is, are)

9. The cereal _____ eaten by my little brother. (was, were)

10. The milk _____ sour. (is, am)

11. In fact, there _____ nothing I want to eat. (is, are)

12. Now I _____ looking forward to lunch! (am, are)

Extension: Have students look through a newspaper or magazine and point out examples of the linking verbs *am, is, are, was,* and *were.*

USING *DO*

Subjects and verbs in sentences must agree in number. In sentences with helping verbs, the helping verb in each sentence must also agree with the subject. *Does*, *do*, and *did* are often **helping verbs**.
Use *does* with the subject *he*, *she* or *it*.
   He does not have a key.
Use *do* with a plural subject or *I* or *you*.
   Mom and Dad do need a key to get into the house. *You do*, too.
Use *did* with a singular or plural subject in the past tense.
   I did want to get in the house. *My sister and brother did*, too.

Read each sentence and the helping verbs in parentheses. Then write the helping verb that correctly completes each sentence.

1. I _____ not know what went wrong. (do, does)

2. This morning I _____ get up very late. (does, did)

3. It _____ seem strange. (do, did)

4. My sister _____ remember getting up late, too. (do, does)

5. We _____ want to get to school on time. (does, did)

6. We _____ have to catch a bus each morning. (do, does)

7. The bus driver _____ wait for us. (do, did)

8. You _____ see us run for the bus. (does, did)

9. Because we were in a hurry, we _____ have to wait now. (do, does)

10. We hope Dad _____ have his key with him. (do, does)

Extension: Have students write *do*, *does*, and *did* on separate cards. Then have each student choose a card and construct a sentence with the helping verb, describing things they do regularly as they come to school.

Macmillan/McGraw-Hill

USING *HAVE*

Subjects and verbs in sentences must agree in number. In sentences with helping verbs, the helping verb must also agree with the subject.

Has, have, and *had* are often helping verbs.

Use *has* with a singular subject and *he, she,* or *it.*
   Ralph has planted vegetables. *He has* watered them well.

Use *have* with a plural subject and *I* or *you.*
   Ed and Mary have helped Ralph. *You have* helped him, too.

Use *had* with a singular or a plural subject in the past tense.
   Ralph had wanted a large garden. *Ralph and his parents had* hoped for a huge garden.

Read each sentence and the helping verbs in parentheses. Then write the helping verb that correctly completes each sentence.

1. Ralph _____ read about gardens. (have, had)

2. He _____ looked at pictures of gardens. (have, had)

3. We _____ talked about gardens. (has, had)

4. Ralph _____ wanted a garden for a long time. (have, has)

5. But he _____ always lived in the city. (have, has)

6. Now Ralph and his family _____ moved to a new apartment. (have, has)

7. They _____ known that the apartment has a balcony. (has, have)

8. Ralph _____ decided to plant a garden on the balcony. (have, has)

9. He _____ put his plants in pots. (have, has)

10. We _____ thought a garden would be great fun. And it is! (has, had)

Extension: Have students write *has, have,* and *had* on separate cards. Have them work in small groups, each choosing a card and constructing a sentence with the word chosen.

Name: _____   Date: _____

BE, DO, HAVE

Be, do, and *have* change form in order to agree with their subjects.

Subject	Verb: *be*		Verbs: *do, have*	
Singular	**Present Tense**	**Past Tense**	**Present Tense**	**Past Tense**
I	am	was	do, have	did, had
you	are	were	do, have	did, had
he, she, it	is	was	does, has	did, had
Plural				
we, you, they	are	were	do, have	did, had

Read each sentence. Write *C* if the sentence is correct. If there is an error, underline the incorrect form of the verb. Then write the correct form. Keep the verb in the same tense as it is now written.

1. Barbara have handed me a plate. _____

2. A piece of cake am on the plate. _____

3. I does like cake. _____

4. You is eating a piece of cake, too. _____

5. I does want just one piece of cake. _____

6. My friends has taken several helpings. _____

7. Barbara's birthday are today. _____

8. I has made something for her birthday. _____

9. We did give a party for Barbara last year. _____

10. She have said that it was a great party. _____

11. This year, I finally did decide what to do. _____

12. Her friends and I has talked about it. _____

13. We am still talking about it. _____

14. I does think we have a super idea. _____

15. We does think of super ideas. _____

Extension: Ask one student to begin a story by saying a sentence that includes one of the verbs listed above. Then have other students add sentences to the story that also include one of those verbs.

Macmillan/McGraw-Hill

MAIN AND HELPING VERBS

Read the following story about an apple tree. Pick out all the rotten apples — mistakes made with main verbs or helping verbs. There are four mistakes in each paragraph. Write the correct verb above the mistake. Be sure the first paragraph is written in the past tense, the second paragraph in the present tense, and the third paragraph in the future tense.

Last fall my grandmother and I planted an apple tree. I has never planted a tree before. I really do help my grandmother plant it. The tree looked like a stick. It do not look as if it would ever grow an apple. We were happy it did grow some leaves before winter. It have not grown any apples.

Now it's springtime. I has gone with my grandmother to look at the tree. It have sprouted new leaves. Several pink-and-white blossoms have started to open. Grandmother and I did not know if the blossoms will turn into apples. We does have hopes for them.

If the blossoms do turn into apples, we will had fun picking them. I will find a basket that will be nice to hold the apples. I will wash the apples. We will has an apple party. We will give apples to all our friends. And we will does something I've always wanted to do. We will has homegrown, homemade apple pie!

Extension: Have students describe something they've grown or would like to grow. Have them describe it using past, present, and future tenses with *have* and *do* as helping verbs.

WHAT IS A MAIN VERB?

A **main verb** tells what the subject does, did, or will do. A **helping verb** aids the main verb in showing an action.

Have, *has*, and *had* are often used as helping verbs.

Use *has* with a singular subject and *he*, *she*, or *it*.

  Tina has offered to help. *She has* told me so.

Use *have* with a plural subject and *I* or *you*.

  Mom and Dad have already gone. *You have* waited long enough.

Use *had* with a singular or plural subject in the past tense.

  Bill and Ted had put up the red tent. *Norm had* borrowed the blue one.

Use *will have* with a singular or plural subject in the future tense.

  I will have done the work.

Draw a line under each helping verb. Circle each main verb.

1. Joseph has made dinner for us before.

2. We have eaten other meals at his house.

3. He had cooked a terrific dinner.

4. But someone had put the salt in the sugar bowl.

5. The soup had tasted very salty because of the mix-up.

6. We have said "no" to using salt ever since.

Write the helping verb and the main verb on the line.

7. Joseph will have invited other people tonight. _____

8. He will have cooked for many hours. _____

9. We will have talked with everyone before dinner. _____

10. Everyone will have looked forward to the dinner. _____

11. Joseph has fixed everything perfectly. _____

12. He has served us a wonderful meal. _____

62 **Extension:** Have students look at the subjects in each of the sentences and decide whether they are singular or plural.

Level 9/Unit 1   12

WHAT IS A HELPING VERB?

A **helping verb** helps a main verb show an action. Forms of *have* and *do* are often used as helping verbs.

We *have* bought lettuce.   We *do* cook every day.

Do cannot be used as a helping verb in the future tense.

Subjects	Helping Verbs: *have, do*		
Singular	**Present Tense**	**Past Tense**	**Future Tense**
I	have, do	had, did	will have
you	have, do	had, did	will have
he, she, it	has, does	had, did	will have
Plural			
we, you, they	have, do	had, did	will have

Draw a line under each helping verb. Circle each main verb.

1. I really do like vegetables.

2. My brothers always have loved pizza.

3. This summer, I did change their thinking.

4. Our family had planted a vegetable garden.

5. We have grown almost all our fresh vegetables.

Write the helping verb and the main verb on the line.

6. My brothers do like fresh radishes and carrots. _____

7. Broccoli has become their favorite vegetable. _____

8. Wonder of wonders, they have tasted spinach. _____

9. I have worked hard in the garden for a good cause. _____

10. Now I will order our favorite food. _____

Extension: Have students use the chart to construct sentences for each of the helping verb forms.

PRACTICE WITH MAIN AND HELPING VERBS

> A **main verb** tells what the subject does, did, or will do. A **helping verb** aids the main verb in showing an action. Forms of *have* and *do* are often used as helping verbs.

Underline the verb that correctly completes each sentence.

1. I (has, had) thought it would be easy to run a store.

2. It (do, does) seem as if anyone could do it.

3. First, I (will have, will has) to find something to sell.

4. Then, you (has, have) to clean and dust the store.

5. You (do, does) have to make your store look nice.

6. People (has, have) got to want to come into the store.

Correct the error in each sentence. First, underline the incorrect verb. Then write the correct verb.

7. So far, you has not sold anything. _____

8. You will has to work harder. _____

9. At last! Someone comes in and do buy something. _____

10. Then you has to ring up the sale. _____

11. You has to wrap up the purchase. _____

12. You can't spend the money yet! I will has to buy more things to sell.

_____

Extension: Have students think about the kind of store they would like to open. Ask them to use the chart of helping verbs on page 63 to construct sentences about the store they are imagining.

Macmillan/McGraw-Hill

MAIN AND HELPING VERBS

Find the errors. First, underline the incorrect form of the verb. Then write the sentence correctly. Keep the verb in the same tense as it is written.

1. Which is the freshest apple? It's the one you has picked from a tree.

_____

2. Tangerines should not be moldy. They does have a bright color.

_____

3. Pears does rot quickly when ripe.

_____

4. Good grapes will not has white spots under their skins.

_____

5. We has waited too long to eat this broccoli. It shouldn't be yellow.

_____

6. Cantaloupe should not have soft spots. It do have a rich scent when ripe.

_____

7. This cauliflower has black spots. We will had to cut them off.

_____

8. I hope you does not eat that green apricot. It is not ripe yet.

_____

9. Tomatoes bruise easily. These must has had a rough trip from the farm.

_____

10. Dates should be shiny and soft. These has just a little mold on them.

_____

Extension: Have students think of their favorite fruits and vegetables. Have them describe them using helping verbs.

LINKING VERBS

Read the following story and then proofread it. There are five mistakes in each paragraph. Write the correct verb above each mistake. Be sure the first paragraph is in the present tense, the second paragraph in the past tense, and the third paragraph in the future tense.

My family am in the army. It are a good thing that we like to travel. We have lived in many different places. This year we are living in Alaska. It am summer now. The days is pretty warm. But I are curious. What is it going to be like in winter?

Last winter we was in Hawaii. Hawaii were a nice place to spend the winter. Sometimes the weather were rainy. But most of the time it were sunny. I were sorry when we left Hawaii.

Our next home are far from Hawaii and Alaska. It are be in the Middle East. Everything was new and strange. We will have to learn a new language. We will learn new customs. But we am happy. Our family are together.

Extension: Have students choose countries in which they would like to live for awhile. Have them describe living in that country using the present, past, and future tenses of the linking verb *be: am, is, are; was, were;* and *will be.*

BE IN THE PRESENT

> **Tense** refers to time. A verb in the **present tense** tells about what is happening now. A **linking verb** does not show action. It connects the subject to the rest of the sentence. The verb *be* has many forms: *am, are, is, was, were, be, been, being.* Use *am* for the present tense when the subject is *I.*
>   *I am* very happy.
> Use *is* for the present tense when the subject is *he, she, it*, or a singular noun.
>   *She is* my good friend.   *Michael is* my best friend.
> Use *are* for the present tense when the subject is *you, we, they*, or a plural noun.
>   *We are* in the same class at school.   *They are* in our class, too.
> Use *are* for the present tense when the subject is a compound.
>   My *brother and sister are* in a different class.

Circle the correct linking verb in each sentence.

1. I (is, am) a gardener.

2. My brother Kimo (is, are) a gardener, too.

3. His garden (is, are) beautiful.

4. The flowers (am, are) all different colors.

5. Kimo and I (is, are) happy.

6. We (is, are) happy in our gardens.

Complete each sentence. Write the correct present-tense linking verb.

7. Roses _____ beautiful flowers.

8. My garden _____ a rose garden.

9. I _____ glad to be here today.

10. All of the roses _____ bright red.

11. They _____ ready to be picked.

12. It _____ a perfect day for gardening.

Extension: Ask students to think of a garden that they have been in or dreamed of being in. Have them use the present-tense linking verbs *am, is,* and *are* to write sentences describing the garden and its flowers.

BE IN THE PAST

Tense refers to time. A verb in the **past tense** tells about what happened in the past. A linking verb does not show action. It connects the subject to the rest of the sentence.
Use *was* for the past tense when the subject is *I, he, she, it*, or a singular noun.
  Kim was eager to start the trip.   Her last *trip was* wonderful.
Use *were* for the past tense when the subject is *you, we, they*, or a plural noun.
  You were with her on that trip.   The *sights were* beautiful.
Use *were* for the past tense when the subject is a compound.
  The *trains and airplanes were* all on time.

Circle the correct linking verb in each sentence.

1. This trip (was, were) almost a disaster.

2. We (was, were) late in starting.

3. Our suitcases (was, were) lost.

4. The weather (was, were) very rainy.

5. The food (was, were) awful.

6. All of us (was, were) miserable.

Complete each sentence with *was* or *were*.

7. The last week of our trip _____ the best.

8. Then we _____ lucky enough to meet Harry.

9. Harry _____ a ranger in Yellowstone National Park.

10. He _____ very happy to help us.

11. The birds and animals _____ right where he said they would be.

12. Everything _____ bright and sunny.

Extension: Ask students to remember a trip they have taken. Ask them to use the past-tense linking verbs *was* and *were* to describe the trip and their feelings about it.

Macmillan/McGraw-Hill

12

Be in the Future

> A verb in the **future tense** tells about what will happen in the future. It uses the verb *will*. The verb *will be* does not show action. It tells about the future and connects the subject to the rest of the sentence.
>
> No matter what the subject of the sentence is, the future tense of *be* is always *will be*.
>
>   *I will be* there.   Our *teacher will be late.*
>
>   *Tomas and Martha will be* with us.   *You will be* at home.

Rewrite each of the following sentences by changing the past or present tense of *be* to the future tense.

1. Our house is right on the beach. _____

2. We are happy living by the sea. _____

3. My uncle and aunt were here on a visit. _____

   _____

4. I was glad to see them. _____

5. All of us were ready for a walk. _____

6. The neighbor's dog is a good swimmer. _____

   _____

7. It always is happy to see us. _____

8. The dog, my aunt, and I were ahead of everyone else.

   _____

9. Seashells are what my aunt and I hope to find. _____

   _____

10. The dog is happy to find a dead fish. _____

   _____

Extension: Ask students to use the future tense of *be* to write sentences describing what walking along a seashore is like.

LINKING VERBS

A **linking verb** does not show action. It connects the subject to the rest of the sentence. The linking verb *be* has different forms.

Subjects	Present Tense	Past Tense	Future Tense
Singular			
I	am	was	will be
you	are	were	will be
he, she, it	is	was	will be
Plural			
we, you, they	are	were	will be

Think of your favorite place in the whole world. Write three sentences about it using the linking verb *be* in each of its present forms at least once.

1. _____

2. _____

3. _____

Write three sentences about your favorite food using the linking verb *be* in each of its past forms twice.

4. _____

5. _____

6. _____

Write four sentences about your favorite thing to do using the linking verb *be* in its future form.

7. _____

8. _____

9. _____

10. _____

70 **Extension:** Ask students to underline each use of *be* in their sentences.

Level 9/Unit 1

10

IRREGULAR VERBS

Read the following story and then proofread it. Find the fifteen errors made with irregular verbs. Write the correct word above the error.

My class goed on a field trip last week. Our teacher tooked us to the zoo. We begun the trip from school. The buses come to pick us up, and we singed all the way to the zoo.

When we gotted to the zoo, we split up into small groups. Each group decided how they would spend their time. My group went to the Lion House. While we were there, we seed the zoo keeper. She feeded the big cats. The zoo keeper gived each animal a helping of fresh red meat. Most of the cats eated their meat right away. The jaguar grabbed its meat and runned away with it.

I have goed to the zoo many times, but I always enjoy it. Everyone had an especially good time last week. I have writed a report about the trip, and I have drawed a picture to go with it. The picture was of the jaguar. I have getted a good grade on the report, and I'm ready to go to the zoo again.

15 Level 9/Unit 1

Extension: Ask students to write a paragraph about teaching someone to fly a kite, catch a fish, or ride a bike. Ask them to use past-tense verbs.

71

IRREGULAR VERBS USING *HAS, HAVE, HAD*: PAST TENSE

Tense shows past, present, or future time. Most verbs form their past tense by adding *ed:* We walk*ed* downtown.

Irregular verbs are verbs that do not add *ed* to form the past tense. These verbs have special spellings.

Verb	Past	Past with *has, have,* **or** *had*
begin	*began*	*has, have,* or *had begun*
come	*came*	*has, have,* or *had come*
do	*did*	*has, have,* or *had done*
eat	*ate*	*has, have,* or *had eaten*
give	*gave*	*has, have,* or *had given*
go	*went*	*has, have,* or *had gone*
grow	*grew*	*has, have,* or *had grown*
run	*ran*	*has, have,* or *had run*

Write the correct form of the verb shown in parentheses in the past tense.

1. I have (grow) _____ an unusual plant.

2. This is the plant I have (give) _____ to you.

3. My sister has (come) _____ to see the plant.

4. She has (go) _____ out of her way to come here today.

5. I have (do) _____ nothing but talk about the plant.

6. My family has (begin) _____ to think I've gone bananas.

7. Actually, I have (go) _____ pineapples.

8. That is the kind of plant we have (come) _____ to see.

9. Wait. Why have you (run) _____ away?

10. What did you say? You have (eat) _____ my plant!

Extension: Ask students to imagine or research one of the plants that we use for food today. Ask them to describe what would happen if that plant became extinct. Remind them to use irregular verbs correctly.   Level 9/Unit 1   10

Macmillan/McGraw-Hill

IRREGULAR VERBS (1): PAST TENSE

Irregular verbs do not add *ed* to form the past tense. These verbs have special spellings to show past tense.

Verb	Past	Past with *has, have,* **or** *had*
bring	*brought*	*has, have,* or *had brought*
draw	*drew*	*has, have,* or *had drawn*
drive	*drove*	*has, have,* or *had driven*
fly	*flew*	*has, have,* or *had flown*
ride	*rode*	*has, have,* or *had ridden*
see	*saw*	*has, have,* or *had seen*
sing	*sang*	*has, have,* or *had sung*
write	*wrote*	*has, have,* or *had written*

Write the correct form of the verb in parentheses. All sentences should be in the past tense.

1. Maria (draw) _____ a picture of the canopy of the rain forest.

2. She also (write) _____ a play about the destruction of the rain forest.

3. Our class (bring) _____ Maria's play to life.

4. We (see) _____ the chance to teach people to care for the forest.

5. Time (fly) _____ by as we worked.

6. Our parents (drive) _____ to school to see the play.

7. We (ride) _____ home feeling great.

8. We (sing) _____ songs that we had written.

8

Level 9/Unit 1

Extension: Ask students to rewrite the sentences with *has, have,* or *had* to show past tense.

73

IRREGULAR VERBS (2): PAST TENSE

Irregular verbs do not add *ed* to form the past tense. These verbs have special spellings to show past tense.

Verb	Past	Past with *has, have,* or *had*
catch	*caught*	*has, have,* or *had caught*
fall	*fell*	*has, have,* or *had fallen*
make	*made*	*has, have,* or *had made*
sit	*sat*	*has, have,* or *had sat*
swim	*swam*	*has, have,* or *had swum*
take	*took*	*has, have,* or *had taken*
teach	*taught*	*has, have,* or *had taught*
throw	*threw*	*has, have,* or *had thrown*

Write the correct form of the verb in parentheses. Each sentence should be in the past tense.

1. James (teach) _____ nine-year-olds last summer.

2. They (come) _____ to a day camp where he was working.

3. First he (give) _____ them each a baseball cap.

4. Then he (take) _____ them to a baseball field.

5. They (throw) _____ baseballs back and forth to each other.

6. Sometimes they (catch) _____ the baseballs.

7. The whole team (sit) _____ on the bench and waited for a turn at bat.

8. No one (fall) _____ off the bench.

Extension: Ask students to rewrite the sentences so that the verbs are in the past tense with *has, have,* or *had.*

Level 9/Unit 1   8

Macmillan/McGraw-Hill

IRREGULAR VERBS

Irregular verbs do not add *ed* to form the past tense. These verbs have special spellings.

Write sentences about the rain forest using the verbs in parentheses. Use the past tense alone and with *has, have*, or *had*.

1. (go) _____

2. (come) _____

3. (begin) _____

4. (run) _____

5. (do) _____

6. (eat) _____

7. (give) _____

8. (grow) _____

9. (see) _____

10. (sing) _____

11. (swim) _____

12. (take) _____

13. (sit) _____

14. (make) _____

Extension: Ask students to read a magazine or newspaper article and underline each use of the past tense of an irregular verb or the past tense with *has, have,* or *had.*

CONTRACTIONS

Proofread the following paragraphs to spot problems with contractions. Each paragraph should have four contractions. Write the correct contraction above the error or above the two words that should be combined.

Our class really would like to do something for our

neighborhood. We arent sure what we should do. We have not

really decided on a project. We can not do anything until we decide.

You wouldnt like to help us, would you?

We should make a list first. Beth can help us. She will write

down all our ideas. Then well choose what we should do. Do not

you think that is a good idea? All right, we are ready to start.

Someone thought of cleaning up the empty lot on the corner. I

am for that. I think thats a good idea. What is your idea? Will not it

be great to do something good for our neighbors?

Extension: Ask students to list as many contractions as they can think of in five minutes. Then have them work with a partner to combine their lists. The pair with the most contractions "wins."

WHAT IS A CONTRACTION?

A **contraction** is a shortened form of two words. An apostrophe (') shows where one or more letters have been left out of a contraction. Some contractions are made from pronouns and verbs. The chart below shows how some contractions are made.

I will = *I'll*	I have = *I've*
you will = *you'll*	I had/I would = *I'd*
he, she, it will = *he'll, she'll, it'll*	you have = *you've*
we will = *we'll*	you had/you would = *you'd*
they will = *they'll*	he, she had = *he'd, she'd*

Write the contraction for the underlined words in each sentence.

1. <u>We will</u> _____ have to get up very early.

2. <u>I have</u> _____ set the alarm clock.

3. <u>You have</u> _____ got to get your things packed.

4. <u>I had</u> _____ hoped we would have found the treasure by now.

5. I know that <u>you had</u> _____ hoped so, too.

6. I am sure <u>you will</u> _____ remember this trip.

7. I know that <u>I will</u> _____ never forget it.

8. <u>I would</u> _____ rather remember it for having found the treasure.

9. If the other team gets there first, <u>they will</u> _____ never forget it.

10. <u>It will</u> _____ take a lot of work to get to the treasure.

10 Level 9/Unit 1

Extension: Ask students to incorporate the contractions from the chart above into a book, movie, or song title, such as *You'll Never Get There from Here.*

77

WITH *BE* (SUBJECT + *BE*)

A **contraction** is a shortened form of two words. An apostrophe (') shows where one or more letters have been left out of a contraction. Some contractions are made with a pronoun and a form of the word *be*. The chart below shows how some contractions are made.

I am = *I'm*	we are = *we're*
you are = *you're*	they are = *they're*
he, she, it is = *he's, she's, it's*	what is = *what's*

Write the contraction for the underlined words in each sentence.

1. <u>I am</u> _____ never going to be late again.

2. <u>We are</u> _____ almost on time today.

3. But <u>you are</u> _____ holding us up.

4. <u>What is</u> _____ the trouble?

5. <u>It is</u> _____ very annoying.

6. <u>They are</u> _____ all waiting for us.

Draw a line under the contraction in each sentence. Then write the two words that make up the contraction.

7. It's not that I want to be late. _____

8. They're always early. _____

9. I'm going to try to change. _____

10. And you're just the person to help me. _____

11. Do you think she's going to be on time, too? _____

12. We're going to get there soon. _____

Extension: Ask students to write a sentence for each of the contractions used in the above chart (eight total).

Macmillan/McGraw-Hill

WITH *NOT*

> A **contraction** is a shortened form of two words. An apostrophe (') shows where one or more letters have been left out in a contraction. A verb and the word *not* can be combined to form a contraction. The chart below shows how some contractions are made.
>
> | | | |
> |---|---|---|
> | is not = *isn't* | does not = *doesn't* | has not = *hasn't* |
> | are not = *aren't* | do not = *don't* | have not = *haven't* |
> | was not = *wasn't* | cannot = *can't* | had not = *hadn't* |
> | were not = *weren't* | will not = *won't* | would not = *wouldn't* |

Write the contraction for the underlined words in each sentence.

1. James <u>has not</u> _____ left for school yet.

2. I <u>do not</u> _____ think he wants to go to school today.

3. <u>Was not</u> _____ his science project due today?

4. <u>Does not</u> _____ he have it finished yet?

5. I <u>cannot</u> _____ help him if he has not finished.

6. I <u>would not</u> _____ be able to help James.

Draw a line under the contraction in each sentence. Then write the two words that make up the contraction.

7. I haven't seen James this morning. _____

8. He wouldn't leave for school without us, would he? _____

9. He isn't here. _____

10. Aren't you worried? _____

11. I hadn't remembered that he was going to leave early. _____

12. Weren't you going to go with him? _____

18 Level 9/Unit 1

Extension: Ask students to make up a set of flashcards with a contraction on one side and the words that make up the contraction on the other side. Show one side of a card to students. Have them write a sentence with whatever form is on the opposite side of the card.

CONTRACTIONS

Rewrite each sentence. Write the contraction for each set of underlined words.

1. <u>Did not</u> you say <u>that is</u> the wrong street?

   _____

2. <u>We will</u> go with you if they <u>are not</u> coming.

   _____

3. <u>What is</u> the problem that <u>they are</u> trying to solve?

   _____

4. <u>Would not</u> Bob like to go when <u>we are</u> going?

   _____

5. <u>She will</u> have to go to the library when <u>I am</u> there.

   _____

6. If you <u>cannot</u> do it, <u>do</u> you <u>not</u> want to go?

   _____

7. <u>You are</u> the best player, <u>are</u> you <u>not</u>?

   _____

8. <u>Has not</u> she found that <u>you will</u> do it for her?

   _____

9. <u>It will</u> have to wait until <u>we are</u> all in the room.

   _____

10. <u>He is</u> the fastest reader, <u>is</u> he <u>not</u>?

    _____

Extension: Ask students to make a poster of rules and safety tips for people who are coming to a park to go swimming, hiking, and camping. Remind them to use contractions in their writing.

Macmillan/McGraw-Hill

PRONOUNS

Proofread the following paragraphs to spot problems with pronouns. You should find five errors in each paragraph. Write the correct pronoun or contraction with a pronoun in it above each error.

Late one spring night, the moon rose slowly in the east. They was a full moon, clear and white. The moonlight filled the desert with bright shadows. It's was as bright as sunshine. Some of the animals played in the moonlight. Them scurried from shadow to shadow. Most of him went about the work of finding food. Them had to find food, no matter how beautiful the night.

The old pack rat sat on her's nest. For such a small animal, the nest was huge. She had been added to bit by bit—a piece of string from here, a sparkly pebble from there. The top of an old tin can was the pack rat's greatest prize. When the moonlight caught the tin just right, she'll shone as bright as a mirror. The sparkle caught the attention of a mother fox and her kits. They've were out looking for food. But the pack rat didn't want to catch their attention. They didn't want to wind up as one of the foxes' snacks.

Macmillan/McGraw-Hill

Extension: Invite students to discuss the kinds of plants and animals found in the southwestern desert. When one student mentions something, the next person should use the correct pronoun in another sentence to add more information.

WHAT IS A PRONOUN?

A **pronoun** is a word that takes the place of one or more nouns. These are some pronouns.

I	*she*	*he*	*him*	*we*	*us*
me	*it*	*you*	*her*	*they*	*them*

Read each pair of sentences. Circle the pronoun in the second sentence. In the first sentence, circle the noun or nouns that the pronoun stands for. Then draw a line connecting the two circles. Finally, write a sentence of your own using each pronoun.

1. My family and I live in the southwest. We live in the desert.

_____

2. My brother likes mountain climbing. He is a good climber.

_____

3. Across the desert, we can see Green Mountain. It is very tall.

_____

4. My brother's class has climbed Green Mountain. They all had a good time.

_____

5. My sister prefers swimming. She is a good swimmer.

_____

6. My sister uses a swimming pool. It is at my sister's school.

_____

7. Our desert doesn't have mountains. It doesn't have a lake either.

_____

8. My family has to drive to the mountains or to a lake. We like driving.

_____

Extension: Ask students to take turns working in pairs. Have them read through a short story in one of their textbooks. The first student finds a sentence with a pronoun in it. Then the second student identifies what the pronoun stands for.

24

Macmillan/McGraw-Hill

SINGULAR PRONOUNS

A **pronoun** is a word that takes the place of one or more nouns. A pronoun may be singular or plural. **Singular** pronouns name a person, place, or thing: *I, you, he, she, it, me, him,* or *her.* When you name a person or other people and yourself in the subject of a sentence, be sure to write about the other person or people first: *Sam and I.*

Underline each pronoun. Write the noun each pronoun takes the place of.

1. "I like the desert," said Maria. _____

2. "Even when the desert is very hot, it is beautiful." _____

3. "I like the desert, too," said Joseph. _____

4. "Would you like to go on a desert hike?" Joseph asked Maria.

_____

5. Maria said she would like to go for a desert hike. _____

6. After Joseph finished speaking, Maria asked him about the hike.

_____

7. Joseph thought about it a moment, then said the hike would not be too

long. _____

8. Joseph then mentioned to Maria that he thought a high school teacher

would lead the hike. _____

9. "The hike would be great if Ms. Lee led it," Maria said. _____

10. "Ms. Lee!" Joseph said. "Oh, I hope so." _____

Draw a line under the correct subject for each sentence.

11. (My family and I; I and my family) went camping.

12. (I and Dad; Dad and I) set up the tent.

Extension: Ask students to form pairs. One student writes a sentence that includes a singular pronoun, and the other student identifies the noun the pronoun stands for.

PLURAL PRONOUNS

A **pronoun** is a word that takes the place of one or more nouns. A pronoun may be singular or plural. **Plural pronouns** name more than one person, place, or thing: *we, you, they, us,* or *them.* Notice that *you* is sometimes singular and sometimes plural. When you name a person or other people along with a group of people in which you are included, be sure to write about the other person or people first: *Sam and we.*

Underline the pronoun in each sentence. Write *S* if the pronoun is singular or *P* if the pronoun is plural.

1. Beth asked Sara, "Have you seen a ring?" _____

2. "No," said Sara. "When did you last see the ring?" _____

3. "When Joseph and I washed the dishes," said Beth. _____

4. "The ring was left on a rock," she continued. _____

5. Joseph added, "It sparkled in the sunlight." _____

6. Beth said, "My parents gave that ring to me." _____

7. "They would be mad if the ring is lost." _____

8. "Both of us have looked everywhere," said Joseph. _____

9. "Do you two think a pack rat could have taken the ring?" _____

10. "We should look near the rock. Pack rats love sparkly things." _____

Draw a line under the correct subject for each sentence.

11. (Beth and we; We and Beth) think a pack rat took the ring.

12. (Sara and we; We and Sara) looked near the rock.

13. (We and Joseph; Joseph and we) found a pack rat's nest.

14. (We and Beth; Beth and we) found Sara's ring.

15. (Beth's family and we; We and Beth's family) were happy to find the ring.

Extension: Ask students to take turns choosing a singular or plural pronoun from the teaching box. Then have the next student complete a sentence using that pronoun correctly.

Level 9/Unit 2   15

Macmillan/McGraw-Hill

CONTRACTIONS WITH PRONOUNS

A **contraction** is a word made up of two words. An apostrophe (') shows where one or more letters have been left out in a contraction. Some contractions are made from pronouns and verbs.

I am = *I'm*	we are = *we're*
I will or shall = *I'll*	we have = *we've*
you are = *you're*	you have = *you've*
he, she, it is or has = *he's, she's, it's*	they are = *they're*
he, she had or would = *he'd, she'd*	they will or shall = *they'll*

Write the contraction for each set of underlined words.

1. <u>She would</u> _____ have fallen asleep.

2. <u>We are</u> _____ the ones who have kept her up.

3. <u>We have</u> _____ been making a lot of noise.

4. <u>She has</u> _____ just about had it.

5. Do you think <u>they will</u> _____ be quieter?

Write two words that each of the following contractions could stand for. Then write a sentence that uses the contraction. Remember to add the apostrophe.

6. he's _____

7. they've _____

8. I'll _____

9. you've _____

10. it's _____

Extension: Ask students to choose five contractions from the chart and use them in sentences.

SUBJECT AND OBJECT PRONOUNS

The pronouns in these two paragraphs are confused. They don't know if they're subjects or objects. Write the correct subject or object pronoun above each mistake. You should find five in each paragraph.

In our class play, me was a radish. Henry, my best friend, was

an apple. You might think that it would be easy to tell we apart.

They would be wrong. An apple and a radish don't look very much

alike. Henry and me don't look alike either. But the biggest laughs in

the play came when Henry got mixed up with I.

The audience loved we. Our voices couldn't even be heard

because people were laughing so hard. The harder we tried to talk,

the harder them laughed. Henry started laughing, too. Him couldn't

stop laughing. Finally, our teacher led Henry and I off the stage. Her

was laughing as hard as anyone.

Extension: Ask students to think about a play or performance they have seen recently. Ask them to write a paragraph describing the actors and the plot. Remind them to use pronouns correctly.

86

Level 9/Unit 2

10

WHAT IS A SUBJECT PRONOUN?

> A **subject pronoun** is a pronoun that is used as the subject of a sentence. The singular (one) subject pronouns are *I, you, she, he,* and *it.*
> The plural (more than one) subject pronouns are *we, you,* and *they.*

Write the subject pronoun in each sentence.

1. Are you a good cook? _____

2. I guess dinner will be the big test. _____

3. It is the first dinner that Mom or Dad hasn't cooked. _____

4. They are looking forward to eating your dinner. _____

5. In fact, we are all excited. _____

Read each pair of sentences. The second sentence in each pair is missing a pronoun. Write the pronoun on the line.

6. Dad cooks dinner at least once a week. _____ usually cooks a stir-fry dinner.

7. There's a farmer's market on Wednesday. _____ has lots of fresh fruits and vegetables to sell.

8. Mom and Dad usually find time to stop at the farmer's market.

   _____ like to shop there.

9. Onions and celery always go into Dad's stir fry. _____ usually has chicken, too.

10. Mom cooks all kinds of good things. _____ also likes to use fresh fruits and vegetables.

10 Level 9/Unit 2

Extension: Ask each student to write three sentences using a singular subject pronoun and three sentences using a plural subject pronoun.

WHAT IS AN OBJECT PRONOUN?

An **object pronoun** is a pronoun that may be used after an action verb in a sentence.
An object pronoun is also used after words such as *for, at, of, with,* and *to.*
The singular object pronouns are *me, you, him, her,* and *it.* The plural object pronouns
are *us, you,* and *them.*

Write the object pronoun in each sentence.

1. Five-year-old Gina made breakfast for us. _____

2. She wanted to make you pancakes. _____

3. She can't cook them yet, though. _____

4. So she made her specialty with me. _____

5. Gina made it with fresh fruits. _____

Read each pair of sentences. Complete the second sentence with the correct
pronoun in parentheses.

6. Gina's mom was the one who discovered Breakfast Delight. She found

   (her, it) _____ in a cookbook.

7. Mom finds lots of good recipes in cookbooks. She reads (her, them)

   _____ all the time.

8. Mom read the Breakfast Delight recipe to Gina and me. She read it to

   (we, us) _____ in the kitchen.

9. Gina listened very carefully to the recipe. Then she wanted Mom to read

   it to (her, she) _____ again.

10. Gina was delighted with Breakfast Delight. She knew that she would

    have fun making it for (we, us) _____.

Extension: Ask each student to write three sentences using a singular object
pronoun and three sentences using a plural object pronoun.

Macmillan/McGraw-Hill

SUBJECT AND OBJECT PRONOUNS

A **subject pronoun** is used as the subject of a sentence to tell what or whom the sentence is about. *I, you, he, she, it, we,* and *they* are subject pronouns.

An object pronoun is used after an action verb or after words such as *for, at, of, with,* and *on. Me, you, him, her, it, us,* and *them* are object pronouns.

Read each sentence. If the pronouns are correct, write *C.* If any pronoun is used incorrectly, rewrite the sentence correctly.

1. The ocean waves knocked down my brother and I.

_____

2. Us had fun trying to swim in the ocean.

_____

3. The lifeguard watched we carefully as them tried to swim.

_____

4. I think she knew that we weren't very good swimmers.

_____

5. My brother and me stopped swimming and walked along the shore.

_____

6. Us looked for shells and found they everywhere.

_____

7. We found shells for our Mom, and we gave it to she.

_____

8. Mom thanked we and told we how pretty them were.

_____

Macmillan/McGraw-Hill

Extension: Ask students to write a paragraph about a favorite person or pet. Then ask a partner to check their writing for the correct use of subject and object pronouns.

USING *I* AND *ME*

> *I* is used in the subject of a sentence. *Me* is used after an action verb or words such as *in, into, with, by,* or *at.*
> *I* like any kind of spaghetti.
> Mom gives *me* meatballs with my spaghetti.
> Sometimes *I* get more spaghetti on *me* than in *me.*

Complete each sentence with *I* or *me.*

1. _____ wanted to learn how to make spaghetti sauce.

2. Mom said she would show _____ how to make it.

3. Mom and _____ made it one afternoon.

4. She helped _____ use tomatoes from our garden.

5. _____ peeled the tomatoes.

6. Then _____ cut them up into small pieces.

7. Mom showed _____ what spices to use in the sauce.

8. She worked with _____ for a long time.

9. _____ cut up onions and mushrooms to put in the sauce.

10. _____ asked Mom to watch it until the sauce was finished.

11. But she had to go to work, so _____ had to finish.

12. The sauce was stirred by _____ for a long time.

13. _____ had to watch it so it wouldn't stick to the pot.

14. The sauce was made by Mom and _____.

15. Thanks to _____, it tasted great!

Extension: Ask students to work in small groups. Have them take turns telling each other about a recent birthday or special day using the words *I* and *me.*

SUBJECT-VERB AGREEMENT

Read the following story about a forest fire. In each paragraph, four mistakes have been made with verbs that have pronouns for subjects. Write the correct verb above each mistake. The first paragraph should be in the past tense, the second paragraph in the present tense, and the third paragraph in the future tense.

Last year, a fire burned this part of the forest. The fire was probably caused by lightning. It will rage out of control for many days. The fire was terrible, but it was a part of nature. People lived near there, so firefighters were called in. They battles the fire as hard as they could. They dug ditches. They dump water on the fire. They try as hard as they could to stop the fire. Finally, the fire was put out, and no lives were lost.

Since the fire, the land looks bare. It seemed like a desert. Tree trunks are black sticks. They stood for a time, but they was not alive. Everything is black. Few plants or animals live here now. They lives where there is more food and shelter.

That will all be changing. Spring will be here soon. Plants will start to grow. They grows from fire-blackened seeds. They will also grow from seeds that have come in from other areas. You see green sprouts here or there. It takes a while, but new plants will grow. Soon insects will come back and then small animals. The forest will grow again. It returns.

12   Level 9/Unit 2

Extension: Ask students to write sentences using the pronouns *he, she, it, I, you, we,* or *they* in the past, present, and future tenses.

91

PRONOUNS WITH PRESENT-TENSE VERBS

A verb in the **present tense** tells what happens now. Add -s to most action verbs in the present when you use a singular noun or the pronouns *he, she,* or *it.*
  It feels like rain. *She takes* her umbrella.
Do not add -s to most action verbs in the present when you use a plural noun or the pronouns *I, we, you,* or *they.*
  Our *dogs hide* from thunderstorms. *They run* under the beds.

Make each verb agree with its subject. Write the correct form of the verb in parentheses on the line.

1. It (rain, rains) whenever we want to play. _____

2. She (want, wants) to go outside. _____

3. I really (want, wants) to play inside. _____

4. We usually (play, plays) together. _____

5. He (live, lives) down the street. _____

6. You (live, lives) right next door to him. _____

7. We (like, likes) playing together. _____

8. I (hope, hopes) it will stop raining. _____

9. Maybe they (know, knows) what to do when it rains. _____

10. She (carry, carries) an umbrella in the rain. _____

Extension: Ask students to list some things they like to do when it rains. Have them write a paragraph in the present tense about one or more of those things. They should use at least four pronouns in the paragraph.

Level 9/Unit 2

10

Pronouns with Past-Tense Verbs

The pronouns *I, you, he, she, it, we,* and *they* are used in the subject of a sentence. These pronouns can be used with past-tense verbs. A verb in the past tense tells what happened earlier. Add *-ed* to most verbs to show past tense. If the verb already ends in *e,* just add *d.*

We walked to soccer practice yesterday.   *I scored* a goal.

Write the past tense for each verb in parentheses. Then use the past tense of the verb and a pronoun in a sentence of your own.

1. Last year, it (snow) _____ a lot. _____

   _____

2. We (love) _____ the snow. _____

   _____

3. It (cover) _____ everything. _____

   _____

4. My dad and I (shovel) _____ the snow. _____

   _____

5. My sister and I (play) _____ in the snow. _____

   _____

6. She (like) _____ to build snow castles. _____

   _____

7. I (enjoy) _____ sledding in the park. _____

   _____

8. You (visit) _____ us last winter. _____

   _____

Macmillan/McGraw-Hill

Extension: Ask students to work in pairs. One student should use one of the verbs on this page in a sentence that has a pronoun and a present- or past-tense verb. The second student then should give the pronoun and tell whether the verb is present or past tense.

Name: _____   Date: _____

PRONOUNS WITH FUTURE-TENSE VERBS

The pronouns *I, you, he, she, it, we,* and *they* are used in the subject of a sentence. These pronouns can be used with future-tense verbs. A verb in the **future tense** tells about what will come or be. It tells about what will happen in the future and uses the special verb *will.*
　　We will go to the movies this weekend.

Write *present* or *past* to show the tense of each sentence. Then rewrite the sentence by changing the past or present tense to the future tense.

1. I prepare for the rain. _____

_____

2. I closed the windows. _____

_____

3. We zip up our raincoats. _____

_____

4. They packed umbrellas for everyone. _____

_____

5. You like the rain. _____

_____

6. I splashed in the puddles. _____

_____

7. He thinks the thunder is too noisy. _____

_____

8. She loves the thunder because it is noisy. _____

_____

Extension: Ask students to list several kinds of storms. Ask them to write a paragraph about what one particular storm will be like. They should use at least four pronouns and the future tense.

94
Level 9/Unit 2
16

Macmillan/McGraw-Hill

SUBJECT-VERB AGREEMENT

> The pronouns *I, you, he, she, it, we,* and *they* are used in the subject of a sentence.
> These pronouns can be used with present–, past–, or future–tense verbs.
> Present-tense verbs tell what is happening now. Add *-s* to most action verbs in the
> present when you use the pronouns *he, she,* or *it*. Do not add *-s* to most action verbs
> in the present when you use the pronouns *I, we, you,* or *they*.
> Past-tense verbs tell what has happened. Add *-ed* to most action verbs to form the
> past tense.
> Future-tense verbs tell about what will come or be. They tell about what will happen in
> the future and use the special verb *will*.

Write the correct tense of the verb called for in parentheses.

1. I _____ the bird to its nest. (past of *follow*)

2. We _____ it feed the baby birds. (future of *watch*)

3. They _____ to be fed a lot. (present of *need*)

4. My sister and I _____ a baby bird. (past of *help*)

5. It _____ very small when we found it. (past of *look*)

6. We _____ our mom what to feed the bird. (past of *ask*)

7. She always _____ what to do. (present of *know*)

8. I _____ we will learn as much as Mom. (present of *hope*)

9. We _____ a lot and learn by reading. (present of *read*)

10. We _____ by doing things, too. (future of *learn*)

10

Level 9/Unit 2

Extension: Ask students to tell about real or made-up experiences with baby
animals. Ask each student to write six sentences—two each in the present, past,
and future tenses—using pronouns to tell about their experiences.

POSSESSIVE PRONOUNS

This Letter to the Editor is about a school library. Proofread the letter, and correct it for publishing. Find four mistakes involving possessive pronouns in each paragraph.

Dear Editor,

Thank you for helping with we book sale. You helped us by

putting free ads in you paper. You wrote articles and told people to

come to us school for the book sale. It helped a lot. We raised over

three hundred dollars for us library.

Our library is one of the best school libraries in the city. It's a

good library because of it librarian. Ms. Marker makes it special.

Mine older brother had Ms. Marker for a librarian. So did mine

sister. Them schoolwork improved because of her work with them.

Ms. Marker has turned kids who don't read into readers. She

has also turned regular readers into great readers. She helps each

student with he's or she's reading. Ms. Marker has had great

success with kids and books. She is successful because she cares

about us books and about us. Thanks again for all yours help.

Sincerely,

Maria Sanchez

Macmillan/McGraw-Hill

WHAT ARE POSSESSIVE PRONOUNS?

> A **possessive pronoun** is a word that takes the place of a possessive noun. It shows who or what owns something. Possessive pronouns do not have apostrophes.
> The singular possessive pronouns are *my, your, her, his,* and *its.*
>   Carol is wearing *her* green coat. *My* coat is green, too.
> The plural possessive pronouns are *our, your,* and *their.*
>   Carol and Mariah are *your* sisters. *Their* coats are red.

Read each sentence. Write the possessive pronoun.

1. My grandmother lives near us. _____

2. I like to visit her house. _____

3. Do your grandparents live near you? _____

4. We have met his grandfather. _____

5. Our grandmother is a special person. _____

6. She is a painter and has painted their picture. _____

7. Her pictures have won many awards. _____

8. She usually paints dogs or cats and their owners. _____

9. Pet owners like the pictures of their pets. _____

10. Each picture shows how special a pet and its owner can be.

    _____

Extension: Ask students to discuss various pets they have owned or known. Have them write a paragraph about one of the pets, using at least three possessive pronouns.

POSSESSIVE PRONOUNS USED BEFORE NOUNS

A **possessive pronoun** is a word that takes the place of a possessive noun. It shows who or what owns something. Sometimes possessive pronouns are used before nouns.
   Our puppy likes to sleep in *your* bed.
The singular possessive pronouns are *my, your, her, his*, and *its*. The plural possessive pronouns are *our, your,* and *their*.

Read each pair of sentences. Complete the second sentence with the correct pronoun. Use the underlined word or words as clues.

1. <u>We</u> went on a tour of the factory.

   (Our, Their) _____ tour was very interesting.

2. Did <u>you</u> go on a tour, too?

   How long did (our, your) _____ tour last?

3. We toured <u>the chocolate cookie factory</u>.

   (Her, Its) _____ cookies are sold everywhere.

4. My <u>sister</u> has always loved those cookies.

   She was sorry that (her, his) _____ class didn't go to the factory.

5. My <u>brother</u> has never liked the cookies.

   He wasn't sorry that (her, his) _____ class missed the tour.

6. <u>We</u> brought a lot of cookies home with us.

   (Our, Your) _____ families enjoyed the cookies we brought home.

7. My sister and brother think about what <u>they</u> eat.

   (Your, Their) _____ eating habits are very good.

8. <u>My</u> family eats a lot of fruits and vegetables.

   (Our, Your) _____ meals are very healthy.

Extension: Help students discuss what makes a meal healthy. Then ask them to write a paragraph about a healthy meal. They should use at least four possessive pronouns.

98

Level 9/Unit 2

8

POSSESSIVE PRONOUNS USED ALONE:
MINE, YOURS, HIS, HERS, ITS, THEIRS

> A **possessive pronoun** is a word that takes the place of a possessive noun. It shows who or what owns something. Some possessive pronouns can stand alone: *mine, yours, hers,* and *theirs.* The possessive pronouns *his* and *its* can be used alone or with a noun.
>
> That mitten is *mine*.   *His* coat is red.   Yes, that's *his*.

Write the correct possessive pronoun to complete each sentence. Use the hints given in parentheses.

1. The red bike is _____. (The bike belongs to a girl.)

2. That glass of milk is _____. (The glass belongs to you.)

3. This ring is _____. (The ring belongs to me.)

4. I think the lost dog is _____. (The dog belongs to a boy.)

5. The new car is _____. (The car belongs to them.)

6. The house on the corner is _____. (The house belongs to you.)

7. Everyone has a book, but that blue book is _____. (The book belongs to a girl.)

8. The package is _____. (The package belongs to them.)

9. The brown coat is _____. (The coat belongs to the dog.)

10. The pencil is _____. (The pencil belongs to me.)

Extension: Ask students to take turns writing sentences in which the possessive pronouns *mine, yours, hers, his, its,* and *theirs* stand alone.

SENTENCE COMBINING WITH POSSESSIVE PRONOUNS

> Sometimes sentences that have possessive pronouns can be combined. You may have to change the verb in the new sentence to agree with the subject.
>
> Your red *scarf is* lost.   My blue *scarf is* lost.
>
> These thoughts or sentences could be combined in different ways.
>
> Our *scarves are* lost.   Your red *scarf* and my blue *scarf are* lost.

Combine each pair of sentences with possessive pronouns. Write your new sentence on the line.

1. My sisters are coming. Your sisters are coming.

_____

2. She likes my dog. She likes your dog.

_____

3. I saw his house. I saw her house.

_____

4. His painting is in the art show. Her painting is in the art show.

_____

5. It's time for your dinner. It's time for my dinner.

_____

6. My bike is red. Their bikes are red.

_____

7. The coat is his. The coat is hers.

_____

8. My book is exciting. Your book is exciting.

_____

Extension: Ask students to rewrite the sentences they wrote in another way. For instance, the first pair of sentences can be combined to read *My sisters and your sisters are coming.* It could also be combined to read *Our sisters are coming.*

Level 9/Unit 2   8

Macmillan/McGraw-Hill

ADJECTIVES

Proofread the following description of a wolf pack. Don't howl if you see a mistake. Write the correct article or adjective above each error. You should find five mistakes in each paragraph.

   Wolves are very socials animals. Being social means that

wolves like others wolves. They live together in family units or

packs. There can be anywhere from two's wolves to fifteen wolves

in an pack. The wolves hunt together, howl together, and take care

of each other. An strongest male is usually the leader of the pack.

   Most wolves mate for life. A female wolf has her babies in late

spring. A baby wolves, or pups, are born in litters of five to

fourteen. The litter usually has seven pups in it. They live in a

underground den for almost a month. When they are about the

month old, they come out and play near the den entrance. A

growns wolf always guards the pups. All members of the pack help

care for the youngs wolves.

Extension: Ask students to choose their favorite wild animal and write a description of it. They should concentrate on using adjectives to make the description vivid and lifelike.

ADJECTIVES THAT TELL *WHAT KIND*

An **adjective** is a word that describes a noun. An adjective can tell what kind of thing the noun is. It is often placed right before the noun it describes.
   A *small* bird is singing in the *tallest* tree.

Underline the adjective in each sentence. Write the noun that the adjective describes on the line.

1. We live in a big city. _____

2. The city has public parks. _____

3. Parks provide quiet places for people. _____

4. Parks have grass and large trees. _____

5. Small children like to play in parks. _____

6. Grown-ups like to be in lovely parks, too. _____

Circle all the adjectives that could describe each underlined noun.

7. This is a _____ park.

   noisy   quiet   with   nice   desk

8. I play here with my _____ friends.

   good   ran   ate   new   old

9. It is cold enough today to wear my _____ coat.

   old   red   wooden   heavy   ceiling

10. My _____ sister is going to the park with me.

   tree   who   younger   little   red-haired

11. First we are going to go for a _____ walk.

   radio   long   quick   chair   telephone

12. Then we are going to sit on a _____ bench.

   green   tree   wooden   paper   comfortable

Extension: Ask students to write about their neighborhood park or one they imagine, using appropriate adjectives.

Macmillan/McGraw-Hill

ADJECTIVES THAT TELL *HOW MANY*

> An **adjective** is a word that describes a noun. An adjective can tell *how many* of
> something there are. *Every, one, some, dozen,* and *ten* are a few of the adjectives that
> tell how many.
>   I would like *two* bowls of soup.

In each sentence, underline the adjective that tells *how many*. Write the noun
that the adjective describes on the line.

1. I know one person who is a great cook. _____

2. She likes cooking every food there is. _____

3. She has written two cookbooks. _____

4. She knows how to make many salads. _____

5. Her favorite meal starts with a dozen clams. _____

6. She likes cooking for eight people. _____

Circle all the adjectives that could describe each underlined noun by telling
how many of something there are.

7. My friend has _____ <u>recipes</u> for cooking chicken.

  six   many   tasty   went   doctor

8. Her best chicken recipe starts with _____ <u>chickens</u>.

  two   some   nobody   cooked   several

9. Then she adds _____ <u>carrots</u>.

  raw   peeled   five   many   baked

10. I've eaten _____ <u>chicken dinners</u>.

  cold   many   some   hot   different

Extension: Ask students to think about their favorite recipes. Challenge them to
write one down, including amounts for each ingredient.

A, An, The

> The words *a, an,* and *the* are special adjectives called **articles**.
> Use *a* before singular nouns that begin with a consonant.
>   *a* snail   *a* flower   *a* cloud
> Use *an* before singular nouns that begin with a vowel.
>   *an* umbrella   *an* apple   *an* orange
> Use *the* before singular and plural nouns.
>   *the* boy   *the* boys   *the* girl   *the* girls

Underline each article. Write the noun that each article points out.

1. I had a dream last night. _____

2. I remember the dream quite clearly. _____

3. My friend and I were riding in an airplane. _____

4. We flew very close to the ground. _____

5. From our plane, I could see an elephant. _____

6. I could also see a tiger. _____

Complete each sentence by writing the correct article.

7. Do you ever remember _____ dreams that you have?

8. I have never had _____ dream quite like this.

9. I hope that I always remember _____ animals that were in it.

10. There was _____ lion as well as a tiger.

11. There was _____ baby elephant as well as grown elephants.

12. One of the strangest animals was _____ anteater.

Extension: Ask students to think about dreams they have had. Ask each student to write about a dream, making sure the articles *a, an,* and *the* are used correctly.

Macmillan/McGraw-Hill

ADJECTIVES

> An **adjective** is a word that describes a noun. An adjective tells what kind or how many.
> *red   wooden   six   several*
> The words *a, an,* and *the* are adjectives called articles. Use *a* before singular nouns that begin with a consonant: *a* car. Use *an* before singular nouns that begin with a vowel: *an* auto.
> Use *the* before singular and plural nouns: *the* train, *the* airplanes.

Circle each article. Then underline each adjective that tells what kind or how many. Write the noun that the article and/or adjective describes on the line.

1. I went to the public library yesterday. _____

2. I always take out six books. _____

3. Yesterday, I found a big book about cats. _____

4. It was the only book that I took out. _____

5. I had a hard time carrying it. _____

6. But I'm having a great time reading it. _____

Add adjectives to each of these sentences. Write each new sentence on the line. Underline the adjectives you added, and draw an arrow to the noun each adjective describes.

7. My brother has a bike.

_____

8. Karen picked the flower.

_____

9. The library has books.

_____

10. Our neighbor walked his dog.

_____

Extension: Ask students to write a short report about a book they have read or one they would like to read. Ask them to concentrate on using adjectives to make their writing more interesting.

Macmillan/McGraw-Hill

ADJECTIVES THAT COMPARE

Proofread this story. Watch for problems with adjectives used to compare.
Write the correct adjective above each mistake. You should find five
mistakes in each paragraph.

Our soccer team this year seems best than last year's team.

Last year our team lost every game we played. It was the more

discouraging year I've ever lived through. We were the sorrier

excuse for a team you can think of. The players ran slower than

snails. Their passes were most off target than you can imagine. We

made fewest goals than I have arms on my body. Do you believe it?

This year our soccer team is going to do much better. We're

going to run faster than last year. Our passes are going to be

straightest. And we're going to make most goals than we've ever

made before. The other teams had better watch out. We're going to

be the faster team ever! We're going to be the hotest team playing!

We've been practicing. We will be much hardest to beat!

Extension: Ask students to think about their favorite game. Have them write a
paragraph about a particular game or player. Emphasize the use of comparative
adjectives.

106

Level 9/Unit 3

10

Macmillan/McGraw-Hill

COMPARATIVE ADJECTIVES: *-ER* OR *MORE*

Add *-er* to an adjective to compare two nouns. When an adjective ends in a consonant and *y,* change the *y* to *i* and add *-er:*   tast*y,* tast*ier*
When an adjective ends in *e,* drop the *e* and add *-er:*   sure, sur*er*
When an adjective has a single vowel before a final consonant, double the final consonant and add *-er:*   fla*t,* fla*tter*
Use *more* to *compare two things.* Never use *more* with an adjective that already has an *-er* or *-est* ending:
    Your sandwich was *more* difficult to make than mine.

Use the correct comparative form of the adjective in parentheses. Write the word on the line.

1. This sandwich is _____ (thin) than any other I have ever seen.

2. It was going to be a _____ (large) sandwich than yours.

3. Do you think you could make a _____ (big) sandwich?

4. Probably anyone could make a _____ (interesting) one.

5. I became a _____ (happy) person as I tried to do just that.

6. I spread a _____ (thick) layer of peanut butter than before.

7. I was also _____ (generous) with the jelly than I had been.

8. What made my second sandwich _____ (strange) than the first?

9. I added a secret ingredient to make it _____ (tasty).

10. My secret ingredient was a banana. It certainly made the sandwich

_____ (yummy) than it had been.

10 Level 9/Unit 3

Extension: Ask partners to take turns playing "Bigger and Better." The first player thinks of an adjective, and the next player uses its comparative form in a sentence and writes the comparative. The partner who spells the most adjectives correctly wins.

SUPERLATIVE ADJECTIVES: *-EST* OR *MOST*

Add *-est* to an adjective to compare more than two nouns. When an adjective ends in a consonant and *y*, change the *y* to *i* and add *-est*:   luc*ky*, luck*iest*
When an adjective ends in *e*, drop the *e* and add *-est*:   safe, saf*est*
When an adjective has a single vowel before a final consonant, double the final consonant and add *-est*:   ho*t*, hot*test*
Use *most* to compare more than two things. Never use *most* with an adjective that already has an *-er* or *-est* ending:
    This is the *most* difficult test I've ever taken.

Use the correct superlative form of the adjective in parentheses. Write the word on the line.

1. Whales are some of the _____ (interesting) animals that have ever lived.

2. The world's _____ (huge) animals might be called exciting or magnificent.

3. It would be difficult to call them the _____ (cute) animals.

4. The blue whale is the _____ (large) living animal.

5. Blue whales eat krill, which are some of the _____ (small) animals in the sea.

6. One of the _____ (sad) things people have done is to hunt some kinds of whales almost to extinction.

7. One of the _____ (happy) things we have done is to stop killing whales.

8. The _____ (likely) place to see a large whale is in the open sea.

9. One of the _____ (lovely) sights in the world is seeing a whale breach, or leap out of the water.

10. Seeing a whale is one of the _____ (exciting) experiences that a person can have.

Extension: Ask partners to take turns playing "Better and Best." The first player thinks of an adjective, and the next player writes a sentence using its superlative form. The partner who spells the most adjectives correctly wins.

Level 9/Unit 3

10

Macmillan/McGraw-Hill

PROOFING PARAGRAPHS WITH ADJECTIVES THAT COMPARE

Add *-er* to an adjective to compare two nouns. Add *-est* to an adjective to compare more than two nouns. Remember to follow spelling rules.
Use *more* to compare two things. Use *most* to compare more than two things. Never use *more* or *most* with *-er* or *-est*.

Proofread this story. Be alert for problems with adjectives used to compare. Write the correct adjective above each mistake. You should find five mistakes in each paragraph.

This year we seem to be having the longer and most coldest

winter I can remember. It's also the snowyest. Yesterday, more

snow fell than had ever fallen before. I started shoveling early in the

day. I shoveled in the middle of the day, and I shoveled at night, too.

It got harder and hardest to shovel the snow. I was more happier at

the beginning of the day when the snow had just started to fall.

I'm hoping that the weather is going to change soon. I'm looking

forward to more brighter and sunniest days. I don't think there's

anything most prettier than a snow-covered place when the snow

has just stopped falling. The sky is blueer. The sun is sunnier.

Everything seems to look loveliest. Trees are covered with

blossoms of white. The world sparkles in the sunlight. And my back

feels better because I don't have to shovel any snow.

Extension: Ask students to recall times when the weather was especially extreme. Have them try to top each other with sentences from imaginary weather reports utilizing *-er, -est, more,* and *most.*

ADJECTIVES THAT COMPARE

Add *-er* to an adjective to compare two nouns. Add *-est* to an adjective to compare more than two nouns. Remember to follow spelling rules.
When an adjective ends in a consonant and *y*, change the *y* to *i* and add *-er* or *-est*.
When an adjective ends in *e*, drop the *e* and add *-er* or *-est*. When an adjective has a single vowel before a final consonant, double the final consonant and add *-er* or *-est*.
Use *more* to compare two things. Use *most* to compare more than two things. Never use *more* or *most* with *-er* or *-est*.

Use the correct comparative or superlative form of the adjective in parentheses. Write the word on the line.

1. That cake is the _____ (flat) cake I've ever seen.

2. The first joke was _____ (funny) than the second joke.

3. This is the _____ (friendly) restaurant in town.

4. Can you imagine writing a _____ (serious) book?

5. Is my apple _____ (large) than your apple?

6. Walking is one of the _____ (healthy) things you can do.

7. Flying an airplane is the _____ (exciting) job I know.

8. Going to the beach is the _____ (relaxing) thing I can think of.

9. An eagle can't fly to _____ (high) places than an airplane.

10. She seemed _____ (happy) than she'd ever been.

ADVERBS THAT TELL *HOW*

Read the following description and correct any mistakes with adverbs. Write the correct adverb above each mistake. You should find five errors in each paragraph.

This morning, we sudden remembered that Molly's birthday was today. We sincerest wanted to make her birthday happy. So we thought very hard about what we could do. I'm not always good at thinking creative. Fortunate, my dad was there to help us. We started to make a birthday cake. Then we eager made cards to give to Molly.

This afternoon, we saw Molly walking slower down the street. She seemed to look sad at me. Happy, I knew that was going to change. Finally, Molly climbed quiet up the stairs. Surprise! We changed her expression. She smiled happiest than I had seen her smile for days. It made us feel great.

Extension: Ask students to think of birthdays or other celebrations and write paragraphs using adverbs that show how the person or people are celebrating and how they are feeling.

What Is an Adverb?

An **adverb** is a word that tells more about a verb. An adverb can be put at the beginning of a sentence, before or after the verb, or at the end of a sentence. Many adverbs end in *-ly*.

Suddenly, I felt cold.

I *suddenly* felt cold.

I felt *suddenly* cold.

I felt cold *suddenly*.

Look carefully for the adverb in each sentence. Then write the adverb on the line.

1. Have you read any good books lately? _____

2. Happily, I've finished cleaning my room. _____

3. Your dog seems to be listening closely to you. _____

4. Bob is waiting eagerly for his birthday. _____

5. Actually, I've been feeling great. _____

6. The tears rolled slowly down his face. _____

7. She does all her work thoroughly. _____

8. The boy looked gratefully at his mother. _____

9. Sue scarcely had time to finish the test. _____

10. I didn't know you could make a dress so quickly. _____

Macmillan/McGraw-Hill

ADVERBS THAT TELL *HOW*

An **adverb** is a word that tells more about a verb. Some adverbs tell how an action takes place. These adverbs usually end in *-ly*.
I walked *slowly* down the hall.

Add *-ly* to each word in parentheses, and use it to complete the sentence. Then write a sentence of your own using that adverb.

1. I woke up _____ this morning. (cheerful)

   _____

2. I could _____ believe my painting had won the prize. (scarce)

   _____

3. Last night, I accepted the prize _____. (grateful)

   _____

4. _____ I wasn't sure that I should have won. (sudden)

   _____

5. I walked very _____ down to breakfast. (quiet)

   _____

6. I _____ talked with my mother about it. (sad)

   _____

7. _____, she made me feel much better. (happy)

   _____

8. I listened _____ to what she had to say. (close)

   _____

Extension: Ask students to imagine themselves as famous painters. Encourage them to think of a scene to paint, and have them write down their thoughts about that scene. Remind them to use adverbs to make their writing lively.

ADVERBS THAT COMPARE *HOW*

Add *-er* to compare two actions. Add *-est* to compare more than two actions.
   Pat got here *faster* than Mary did.   Pat walks *fastest* when she is on her way home.
Use *more* and *most* to form comparisons with adverbs ending in *-ly*. Use *more* to compare two actions. Use *most* to compare more than two actions.
   Pat moves *more rapidly* than I do.   In our class, Pat walks the *most rapidly* of anyone.

Decide whether to use *-er, -est, more,* or *most* to make the correct form of the adverb in parentheses. Write the sentence correctly on the line.

1. Who can bark (loud), your dog Sam or my dog Tiger?

   _____

2. We both know that Tiger can bark (loud) than Sam.

   _____

3. Between Tiger and Sam, Tiger runs (quickly), too.

   _____

4. Tiger works (hard) than Sam and learns new tricks.

   _____

5. Tiger learns (quick) of any dog on the block.

   _____

6. Of all the dogs I know, Tiger learns (fast).

   _____

7. But of all the dogs I know, Sam loves me (completely).

   _____

8. Of all the dogs in the world, it's Sam who comforts me (wholeheartedly).

   _____

Extension: Ask students to take turns comparing two animals by using adverbs with the *-er* and *-est* endings, as well as adverbs with the words *more* and *most*.

ADVERBS THAT TELL HOW

> An **adverb** is a word that tells more about a verb. Some adverbs tell *how* an action takes place. These verbs usually end in *-ly*.
> Add *-er* to compare two actions. Add *-est* to compare more than two actions. Use *more* and *most* to form comparisons with adverbs ending in *-ly*. Use *more* to compare two actions. Use *most* to compare more than two actions.

Add *-ly* to each word in parentheses, and use it to complete the sentence. Then write a sentence of your own using a form of that word to compare how something happened. Be sure to use *-er, -est, more,* and *most* at least once.

1. I ran _____ of anyone in my class. (quick)

_____

2. The painters _____ had time to finish the walls. (scarce)

_____

3. She _____ tells me not to do that. (constant)

_____

4. Lately, I've been seeing birds _____ than before. (often)

_____

5. I _____ couldn't think of the words to the song. (sudden)

_____

6. Bob put the dishes away _____ than the last time. (careful)

_____

7. Of all the skaters on the ice, Hakim skated _____. (graceful)

_____

8. Sarah skates _____ than I do. (fast)

_____

Macmillan/McGraw-Hill

16

Level 9/Unit 3

Extension: Ask students to think of an experience that they would like to have and then brainstorm a series of adverbs to describe what is happening.

115

ADVERBS THAT TELL *WHERE* AND *WHEN*

Write a paragraph about a dream you had recently. Include descriptive words that help to explain exactly what happened. Use at least five adverbs that tell *when* or *where* something happened.

_____

_____

_____

_____

_____

_____

_____

_____

_____

_____

_____

_____

_____

_____

_____

_____

_____

ADVERBS THAT TELL *WHERE*

An **adverb** is a word that tells more about a verb. Some adverbs tell where an action takes place. Adverbs that tell where include *there, outside, up, here, nearby, ahead, around, far, away,* and *everywhere.*

Underline the adverb in each sentence. Then use the adverb in a sentence of your own, and write it on the line.

1. I would love to go there with you.

_____

2. The whole family has been working outside.

_____

3. I looked everywhere but didn't find the cats.

_____

4. Nearby is a small town that we can visit.

_____

5. Would you like to come here and study?

_____

6. They are going up to look in the attic.

_____

7. The bend in the road is just ahead.

_____

8. The small dog ran around chasing its tail.

_____

Macmillan/McGraw-Hill

16 Level 9/Unit 3

Extension: Ask students to brainstorm as many other adverbs that tell *where* as they can. If they have trouble deciding whether a word is or is not an adverb, encourage them to check a dictionary.

ADVERBS THAT TELL *WHEN*

> An **adverb** is a word that tells more about a verb. Some adverbs tell when an action takes place. Adverbs that tell when include *first, always, next, later, tomorrow, soon, early, today, then,* and *yesterday.*

Underline the adverb in each sentence. Then use the adverb in a sentence of your own, and write it on the line.

1. Will we go to the store tomorrow?

_____

2. First, I am going to tell you a story.

_____

3. This story always has a happy ending.

_____

4. A young girl woke early in the morning.

_____

5. Next, she went to make breakfast.

_____

6. Soon, she was eating cereal and toast.

_____

7. That's what she always eats.

_____

8. Then she heard her dog barking.

_____

Extension: Ask students to brainstorm as many other adverbs as they can that tell *when.* If they have trouble deciding whether a word is or is not an adverb, encourage them to check a dictionary.

Macmillan/McGraw-Hill

ADVERBS THAT COMPARE *WHERE* OR *WHEN*

> An **adverb** is a word that tells *how, when,* or *where.* Add *-er* or use *more* when two actions are compared.
> Add *-est* or use *most* when more than two actions are compared.

Correct the adverbs that compare in each sentence. Rewrite each sentence correctly on the line.

1. Jane's sister always wakes up earliest than Jane does.

_____

2. I arrived later of all my friends.

_____

3. Of all the biology students, Henry peered more closely at the insect.

_____

4. The turtle crossed the finish line soonest than the hare.

_____

5. If we don't hurry, we'll arrive at the game latest than last time.

_____

6. Of the whole team, Mary can throw the ball more farther.

_____

7. I hope the letter carrier comes soonest than she did yesterday.

_____

8. The principal usually arrives more earlier than the students.

_____

Extension: Ask students to recall a play or a program they have seen recently.
Ask them to write a brief review of the event, using adverbs that compare.

ADVERBS THAT TELL *WHERE* AND *WHEN*

An **adverb** is a word that tells more about a verb. Some adverbs tell where or when an action takes place. Two actions can be compared by using -*er* and *more*. More than two actions can be compared by using -*est* and *most*.

Revise each sentence by adding adverbs that tell where and when the action takes place. Write your sentence on the line.

1. The bus stopped.

_____

2. We went to camp.

_____

3. They ate breakfast.

_____

4. Our dog waited for us.

_____

5. We will drive.

_____

Revise each sentence by correcting any mistakes in adverbs that compare. Write your sentence on the line.

6. She goes to the bus stop more earlier than anyone else.

_____

7. Of everyone playing tag, David runs farther away.

_____

8. He finished the book most soonest than Steve or Erin.

_____

Extension: Ask students to choose a picture from a magazine. Ask them to use at least two adverbs that tell *how*, two adverbs that tell *where*, and two adverbs that tell *when* as they write a description of the picture.

120

Level 9/Unit 3

8

Macmillan/McGraw-Hill